# LUNCH BOX

This book is dedicated to all the parents, children, wives, husbands, partners, guardians and grandparents who strive to give themselves and their loved ones the ultimate gift of nutrient-dense food. This is what allows us, as humans, to thrive. Never underestimate the power a great lunch can have on one's body, mind and spirit.

Cook with love and laughter,

Pete xox

70+ HEALTHY MEALS, SNACKS
& TREATS FOR ON THE GO

# LUNCH BOX

## PETE EVANS

dairy free • gluten free • nut free • refined-sugar free

# CONTENTS

# INTRODUCTION

I have wanted to put together a cookbook on healthy packed lunches for such a long time now, as I feel it is so important for anyone who is passionate about good health. Finally, I can tick it off my bucket list! This book is for anyone looking for nutritious, delicious and relatively easy recipes for their families' lunch boxes – for childcare, primary school or high school – or for themselves and their household to take to work.

Ever since the introduction of our so-called healthy eating guidelines several decades ago, which encourage us to eat up to ten serves of grains and/or cereals per day, our health has taken a huge downward turn. All you need to do is look at what people are putting in their lunch boxes these days, or buying from food courts, drive-throughs or cafes, to see how far removed we have become from natural, nutrient-dense fuel for our bodies. We are encouraged to eat five serves of vegetables a day. Now, how can that possibly happen when most people's diets look a little like this?

- **Breakfast:** toast or cereal (no veggies)
- **Morning tea:** a muffin, muesli bar or fruit (again, no veggies)
- **Lunch:** a roll, wrap or sandwich or perhaps some sushi (very little veggies, if any)
- **Afternoon tea:** coffee, chocolate or nuts (again, no vegetables)
- **Dinner:** a side of vegetables – if you're lucky, even if you're a vegetarian!

There is, however, a very simple alternative and it starts with re-thinking the way we eat breakfast. Try having some protein-rich meat, seafood or eggs with a side of vegetables and some good fats, which will then make it so much easier to fuel yourself through to lunch. Or perhaps you can fast for breakfast (if you don't have any blood-sugar issues), then have a delicious power-packed lunch using any one of the recipes in this book. Once you eat a lunch like this, it should be enough to see you flying through to dinner time, without the need for snacks or coffee and without the dreaded afternoon slump.

Children, in particular, need this simple formula of protein + healthy fats + veggies to help them thrive in their school years. That is why I believe this to be the most important book I have ever written, and the one I am proudest of, because if we can set up good eating habits for our children now, then we have the opportunity to change our nation's health for the coming generations. The way we teach our kids to eat and nourish their bodies will have a profound, flow-on effect for their own children, who will hopefully be stronger and more robust than the current generation, who are suffering chronic illness like never before.

The philosophy behind this book is a low-carb, healthy-fat approach steeped in paleo principles (or, as you might like to call it, an anti-inflammatory diet). Paleo is about eliminating refined sugars and inflammatory foods, such as grains, legumes and dairy, from our diets. Instead, a paleo diet is based around plenty of seasonal, spray-free or organic veggies and a moderate amount each of good-quality fats and protein – all of which are emphasised in the recipes in this book. Note that I have taken care to remove nuts from almost all of these recipes, as I know that many schools are nut-free zones these days, but please feel free to add them to your own lunches if you choose to.

I see no difference between school lunches for kids and work lunches for adults, except for the portion sizes, so all of the recipes in this book have been designed for both. It makes so much more sense for kids to be eating the same food as their parents – and saves doubling up on the cooking and prepping too! My advice is to cook up a double or triple batch of the meals in this book. You can freeze them for later use or simply pack the same lunch a couple of days in a row, or just eat any extra portions for breakfast or dinner at home on other days. Please use these recipes as guides only, and feel free to adapt them to suit your own tastes, skills, budget and local resources. Have fun with my recipes by putting your own spin on them.

A simple formula I like to use at home for my girls' school lunches is:

one serve of organic, seasonal fruit + raw or cooked seasonal, organic veggies + protein and fat in the form of meat, seafood and/or eggs

It really doesn't need to be any more complicated than that! If you like, you can pack a healthy treat (see pages 145–165) though note that I see these as 'sometimes foods' for special occasions, such as school fetes, birthday parties or office baking fundraisers, so that you and your family don't feel left out. Perhaps you can even educate others with your knowledge and healthy, delicious food! And if you feel the need to include bread or crackers, simply make some of our grain-free and nut-free options on pages 39–57. Add to this some freshly filtered water and you have all the makings of a perfect healthy lunch.

I also encourage you and your family to consume some bone broth during the week, as well as small daily amounts of fermented vegetables and beverages, such as coconut kefir and kombucha, for good gut health. These are a little trickier to add to lunch boxes, so just have some with breakfast or when you get home from work or school.

Remember that if children don't like a particular flavour or texture, research suggests that by the tenth time of trying something they can begin to appreciate the new ingredient or dish. It is all about leading by example and trying your best not to allow kids to develop a taste for the boring, beige foods that are so prevalent these days: refined grain foods such as bread, pasta, rice, oats and all wheat-based products. They really have no flavour and are causing so many issues for our bodies and the environment.

Lastly, I would like to thank you for your commitment to your own health and that of your family, and also for doing your bit to help ease the load on the nation's health system and contribute to a healthier environment for the coming generations. Never underestimate how powerful your choice to create one healthy meal after another for yourself and your family is; through this thoughtful act of self-love and love for your family, you are actually creating change, as your actions will influence so many people around you. Even though you might feel you are swimming against the tide sometimes, always remember that the tide will eventually change.

Keep cooking with love and laughter,
Pete xox

# TOP TIPS FOR A SAFE AND HEALTHY PACKED LUNCH

What are the essential things to keep in mind when selecting food-storage products for packed meals for school, work or travel? There is now such an extensive range of products in the market that buying the right ones can get confusing. Below is a guide to help you choose the best food-storage products for you and your family, including food-safety tips for keeping prepared and packaged meals safe from toxic chemicals and, most importantly, from harmful bacteria growth that can occur when food is not stored in the proper way.

## What to look out for when purchasing lunch boxes and drink bottles

Most lunch boxes and drink bottles these days are made from plastic, and it's hard to tell which plastic is leaching out dangerous chemicals. Most of the softer, bendy plastic food containers contain PVC, which is a toxic material that releases dioxin and phthalates when manufactured and in use. Harder plastic lunch boxes and bottles often contain Bisphenol A (BPA), which also releases toxic chemicals into food and drinks when in use.

Always look at the labels on lunch boxes and drink bottles to check what materials they are made from. Avoid PVC and BPA at all costs. If the label doesn't specify any materials, it's best to avoid it completely. If you look at the bottom of your plastic container, you will usually see a triangular recycling symbol containing a number from 1 to 7. Number 3 is PVC, number 6 is polystyrene and number 7 is polycarbonate. If you see any of these three numbers on the product, it's best to avoid.

Some lunch boxes and drink bottles labelled 'BPA free' are still not necessarily safe, as many manufacturers are now replacing BPA with Bisphenol S (BPS), which is turning out to be worse. Often a dangerous chemical is banned or phased out only to be replaced with one that is equally as bad.

When purchasing lunch boxes and drink bottles, I highly recommend choosing stainless steel, tempered glass or silicone, as these materials are antibacterial and do not leach chemicals into food or liquid. More and more companies are making these types of easy-to-pack lunch boxes and storage containers in all shapes and sizes, often featuring bento-style compartments to keep food separated and leak-free lids to keep meals fresh.

If you have previously been using plastic containers at home to store food, you don't have to toss them all in one go, but try to slowly start replacing them with glass, stainless steel or silicone containers.

Below is a list of websites where you can find a range of non-toxic and eco-friendly products:

- Biome.com.au
- Honeybeewrap.com.au
- House.com.au
- Lunchbots.com
- Planetbox.com
- Thermos.com.au

The rule to remember is to avoid plastic. Wrapping your lunch in baking paper or reusable beeswax paper (also handy for covering food for the fridge) and using a brown paper bag is the best way to pack your lunch if you do not have containers.

## Thermoses

Thermoses are insulated containers that are designed to keep meals and beverages such as soups, curries, stews, tea and coffee hot for up to six hours. They can also keep food and beverages such as salads, yoghurts, iced teas and juices cold for up to 10 hours.

Thermoses have stainless steel interiors and exteriors, and are easy to clean and practically unbreakable. Their screw-top lids are leak-proof to prevent spillage and to keep the contents well insulated. It's always best to read manufacturer instructions before use to ensure you get the full benefits out of your thermos.

## Food safety

Packing lunch for yourself or your children by preparing healthy meals and snacks from scratch or by using up leftovers from the night before is a great way to ensure a nutritious meal. However, if food is not treated and stored correctly, harmful bacteria can multiply very quickly and lead to food poisoning.

Here are a few safety tips:

- Always wash your hands thoroughly with soap and warm water before preparing food.
- Ensure cutting boards, benches and utensils are clean and dry.
- Wash fruit and vegetables thoroughly before use.
- Wash cutting boards, dishes and benchtops with hot, soapy water after preparing each food item and before moving on to the next. This will prevent cross-contamination.
- When refrigerating lunch-box items, ensure they're well covered and separated from other foods – especially raw meats.
- Keep lunch-box items in the fridge for as long as possible, removing them from the fridge the moment you or your child leave home for work or school.
- Keeping packed perishable food items chilled is very important, even on the coldest days. This will prevent harmful bacteria from multiplying if the temperature is between 5°C and 60°C. It is highly recommended to store lunch boxes or containers in insulations bags with ice-bricks when transporting, and then refrigerate upon destination if possible.
- If refrigeration is not available at school or work, arrange perishable foods between ice blocks and pack in cooler bags until consumed.
- Frozen water or juice bottles can also be used as freezer packs. Prepare and freeze the night before, then pack in insulated bags in the morning or before travelling. After a few hours in the bag, it should be thawed and ready to drink.
- It is safe to prepare lunches the night before as long as they are stored in a fridge or freezer. Don't pack anything that has just been cooked or is still warm. Food must be well chilled before packing.
- Once home from school or work, throw out all perishable items that have not been consumed.
- Throw away any food containers that are cracked, broken or noticeably scratched.

# FREEZER-FRIENDLY LUNCHES

Preparing food for school or work lunches can sometimes get a little challenging, especially on those busy mornings when you're trying to get everyone out the door before rush hour. I have designed this book to include many freezer-friendly recipes, so why not make a big batch of meals on the weekend – such as meaty muffins, sausage rolls or banana bread – and have them individually portioned, securely wrapped or packed into airtight containers and stored in the freezer? These meals can be made well in advance and stored frozen for up to 3 months or more.

When it's time to start making lunches in the morning, simply pop the frozen meals straight from the freezer into lunch boxes. By lunchtime they will be thawed and ready to eat or reheat. This is a great way to keep perishable food at a safe temperature, and make those busy mornings so much easier.

Here is a list of dishes from this book that you can make and freeze in advance. Note that this means the main component of the dish can be frozen, not necessarily the sides:

TOASTED SPICED SEEDS
SMOKY COCONUT CHIPS
FLAX OR CHIA EGG REPLACEMENT
BACON AND EGG FAT BOMBS
AVOCADO DIP
ROSEMARY SEED CRACKERS WITH CHICKEN AND MAYONNAISE SALAD
FLAXSEED CRACKERS WITH TUNA
COLESLAW
SWEET POTATO HUMMUS
CRISPY PORK CRACKLING
VEGETABLE CRISPS
GREEN JUICE
KETOGENIC CHOC–BERRY SMOOTHIE

With nut allergies so prevalent, nut restrictions in schools and childcare centres need to be taken very seriously. However, this is no reason for our kids to miss out on nourishment and textural mouthfeel. Seeds are an excellent alternative to nuts and, in some cases, offer an even better nutritional profile. Here is a really simple recipe that can be made in bulk and stored. These spiced seeds can be eaten on their own or sprinkled onto salads, soups, stews, curries, stir-fries, breakfast dishes and pretty much anything savoury.

# TOASTED SPICED SEEDS

## MAKES 400 G

50 g (⅓ cup) flaxseeds
150 g (1 cup) pumpkin seeds
150 g (1¼ cups) sunflower seeds
1½ tablespoons sesame seeds
2 tablespoons coconut oil
2 teaspoons ground cumin
1 teaspoon ground coriander
3 teaspoons ground turmeric
pinch of cayenne pepper
1 teaspoon honey (optional)
2 teaspoons tamari or coconut aminos*
¼ teaspoon fine sea salt

* See Glossary

Place the flaxseeds in a bowl, pour over enough water to cover by at least 2 cm and leave for 30 minutes.

Preheat the oven to 160°C (140°C fan-forced). Line a large baking tray with baking paper.

Drain the flaxseeds (they will have a gelatinous texture) and place in a large bowl. Add the remaining ingredients and mix well to combine.

Evenly spread the seed mixture over the prepared tray in a single layer and bake for 20–25 minutes until dry and golden. Allow to cool and store in an airtight container in the pantry for up to 1 month.

Coconuts contain an amazing amount of healthy fat, which is why they are one of my all-time favourite foods to include in my family's diet. Everything from the cream, milk and water to the flesh can be used in so many different ways. If you're looking for a fun, relatively cheap and super-delicious snack that will keep the family happy, then look no further than these crunchy and chewy coconut chips. They also make a great topping for soups, curries, eggs and other savoury dishes.

# SMOKY COCONUT CHIPS

## SERVES 3–4

2 tablespoons tamari or
   coconut aminos*
1½ tablespoons maple syrup
½ teaspoon smoked paprika
90 g (1⅓ cups) coconut chips

* See Glossary

Preheat the oven to 150°C (130°C fan-forced). Line a baking tray with baking paper.

Place the tamari or coconut aminos, the maple syrup and smoked paprika in a bowl and mix to combine. Gently toss through the coconut until well coated and leave to marinate for 5 minutes.

Spread the marinated coconut over the prepared tray in a single layer and bake, stirring gently every 5 minutes or so, for 10–13 minutes until golden. Keep a close eye on the coconut after 10 minutes, as it can quickly burn. Allow to cool completely before serving. Store in an airtight container in the pantry for up to 2 weeks.

Many classrooms these days are egg-free zones due to allergies, so this egg replacement recipe is a good one to have up your sleeve when making school lunches. It's perfect to use in fish or meat muffins (see recipes pages 66–85), banana bread, cookies and other baked goods, but not for egg-based muffins as they will become dense and chewy after baking.

# FLAX OR CHIA EGG REPLACEMENT

**MAKES 3 TABLESPOONS**

1 tablespoon freshly ground flaxseeds
   or chia seeds
3 tablespoons filtered water

Place the ground flaxseeds or chia seeds in a bowl, add the filtered water and whisk well to combine. Allow to sit for 15 minutes to develop a gelatinous texture, similar to an egg.

**Notes**

3 tablespoons of flaxseed or chia egg replacement equals 1 egg.

You can make this in large quantities and store in the fridge for up to 1 week.

One of the most common questions I get asked is what to feed hungry teenagers. This recipe really comes in handy and will keep teenagers – as well as the rest of the family – happy and full between meals. It's a great idea to whip up a big batch of these on the weekend so you can direct the family to the fridge to get their fat fix throughout the week, and you can feel good knowing they'll be satiated until mealtime. These make great lunch-box additions alongside some fresh or cooked vegetables and sauerkraut.

# BACON AND EGG FAT BOMBS

## MAKES 10

6 rindless bacon rashers
4 large hard-boiled eggs, peeled
70 ml coconut oil or good-quality animal fat*, melted
80 g Mayonnaise (page 174)
1½ tablespoons chopped flat-leaf parsley leaves
sea salt and freshly ground black pepper
veggie sticks, to serve (optional)

* See Glossary

Preheat the oven to 200°C (180°C fan-forced). Grease and line a baking tray with baking paper.

Arrange the bacon on the prepared tray in a single layer, making sure the strips are not touching. Bake, turning the tray once for even cooking, for 15–20 minutes until the bacon is golden and crisp. Keep a close eye on the bacon to prevent it from burning. Set aside until needed and reserve the bacon fat for the egg mixture.

Mash the eggs in a bowl, then add the oil or fat, the reserved bacon fat, the mayonnaise and parsley. Mix gently until combined. Season with salt and pepper. Cover with plastic wrap and refrigerate for 30 minutes.

Meanwhile, chop the bacon into small pieces ready for rolling.

Remove the egg mixture from the fridge and roll into ten walnut-sized balls. Roll each ball in the bacon bits to coat, then place on a tray and refrigerate for 20–30 minutes until slightly firm. Enjoy the fat bombs on their own or serve with a side of veggie sticks, if desired.

We can all agree that avocados are a healthy and delicious inclusion in our diets. How you choose to incorporate them into your meals is completely up to you. We love avocado in smoothies, desserts and for breakfast on paleo bread or seed crackers; and it is lovely piled on top of a burger or paleo nachos or served on the side of a piece of fish.

When avocados are bountiful, cheap and in season, you could make a big batch of this dip and freeze it in smaller containers so that you always have some on hand to serve with fresh veggies as we have done here. Or you can simply spread it on seed crackers (page 46) or use it in sandwiches.

# AVOCADO DIP

## SERVES 4

2 avocados, stones removed
1 ½ tablespoons lemon juice
60 g (¼ cup) Aioli (page 168) or
    Mayonnaise (page 174)
sea salt and freshly ground
    black pepper
1 tablespoon finely chopped basil
    leaves, plus extra leaves to serve
1 tablespoon extra-virgin olive oil

### To serve
1 large carrot, cut into 8 cm sticks
1 celery stalk, cut into 8 cm sticks
1 red capsicum, cut into 8 cm sticks
100 g Sauerkraut (page 177)

Mash the avocado with a fork or potato masher until creamy but still slightly chunky. Add the lemon juice and aioli or mayonnaise and mix until combined. Season to taste with salt and pepper.

Mix together the chopped basil and oil to combine, then mix half the basil oil through the avocado mixture.

Spoon the avocado dip into a serving dish and drizzle over the remaining basil oil, add a pinch of salt and pepper and scatter over the extra basil leaves. Serve with the vegetable sticks and sauerkraut.

When we cook a glorious roast chook at home, we generally eat about half of it and then enjoy the other half as leftovers for days to come. We use the leftovers in soups, salads, bhajis and omelettes, or make a yummy chicken and mayonnaise salad like this, which is just perfect between slices of paleo bread or dolloped on seed crackers.

# ROSEMARY SEED CRACKERS WITH CHICKEN AND MAYONNAISE SALAD

## SERVES 4

### Rosemary seed crackers

30 g (¼ cup) sunflower seeds
75 g (½ cup) pumpkin seeds
1½ tablespoons freshly ground flaxseeds
2 teaspoons psyllium husks*
2 teaspoons finely chopped rosemary
¼ teaspoon fine sea salt
3 tablespoons filtered water
1½ tablespoons coconut oil or
   good-quality animal fat*, melted
1 egg
tapioca flour*, for dusting
olive oil, for brushing
flaky sea salt, for sprinkling

### Avocado puree

1 avocado, stone removed
1 tablespoon lemon juice

### Chicken and mayonnaise salad

200 g cooked chicken, shredded
80 g Mayonnaise (page 174)
1 teaspoon lemon juice
1 teaspoon chopped tarragon leaves
1 teaspoon finely chopped curly or
   flat-leaf parsley leaves
sea salt and freshly ground black pepper

### To serve

1 baby cos lettuce, finely shredded
2 radishes, cut into matchsticks
1 small handful of chervil sprigs
extra-virgin olive oil

* See Glossary

Preheat the oven to 200°C (180°C fan-forced).

To make the crackers, combine the sunflower seeds, pumpkin seeds, flaxseed, psyllium husks, rosemary and salt in the bowl of a food processor and process to a fine powder. Add the water, the coconut oil or fat and the egg and continue processing until the dough comes together to form a slightly wet and sticky paste. Transfer the dough to a work surface dusted with tapioca flour. Roll into a ball, place on a large sheet of baking paper and pat down to flatten into a disc. Allow to rest for 10 minutes. Place another large sheet of baking paper over the flattened dough and, using a rolling pin, roll out to a thickness of 2 mm. Peel away the top sheet of paper and discard. Using a pizza cutter or sharp knife, cut into rectangles or your desired shape and size. Transfer the dough shapes and the baking paper to a baking tray. Brush the shapes with a light coating of olive oil and sprinkle with the flaky salt. Bake, turning the tray halfway through, for 25–30 minutes until golden. Allow to cool completely before removing from the tray and serving. Store in an airtight container in the pantry for up to 1 week.

To make the avocado puree, place the avocado and lemon juice in the bowl of a food processor and blend until smooth and creamy. Season with salt and pepper. Transfer to a bowl and set aside until needed.

To make the chicken and mayonnaise salad, place the chicken, mayonnaise, lemon juice and chopped herbs in a bowl and mix well to combine. Season with salt and pepper.

Place the rosemary seed crackers on a platter and top each with some lettuce, then dollop on a tablespoon of avocado puree and a spoonful of chicken and mayo salad. Scatter on the radish and chervil, drizzle on some extra-virgin olive oil and serve.

When adopting the paleo lifestyle, don't ever worry that you'll be missing out on the things you love to eat. We are all about adapting recipes that contain the most common inflammatory ingredients (gluten, grains, legumes, dairy and refined sugars). Here, we have healthy crackers that taste so much better than any commercially made wheat- or rice-based versions. Once you have made these, try them topped with your favourite paleo dip or spread – or why not whip up a seafood spread like this? You could also use sardines, salmon, mussels or smoked eel instead of the tuna (see Note page 90).

# FLAXSEED CRACKERS WITH TUNA

## SERVES 2

185 g tuna in brine*, drained
3 tablespoons lemon-infused olive oil
zest of ½ lemon
sea salt and freshly ground
    black pepper
1 teaspoon chopped dill fronds

## Flaxseed crackers

160 g (1 cup) golden or brown
    flaxseeds
80 g (⅔ cup) mixed seeds
    (such as pumpkin, sunflower
    and sesame seeds)
½ teaspoon sea salt
½ teaspoon of your favourite spice
    (such as curry powder, smoked
    paprika, ground cumin or
    fennel seeds) (optional)

## To serve

80 g Mayonnaise (page 174) or
    Aioli (page 168)
2 semi-hard-boiled eggs, halved
1 celery stalk, cut into sticks
6 truss or heirloom cherry tomatoes
lemon slices

* See Glossary

To prepare the flaxseed crackers, place the flaxseeds in a bowl, pour over enough water to cover and leave overnight. Place the mixed seeds in a separate bowl, pour over enough water to cover and leave overnight.

The next morning, drain and rinse the mixed seeds. Drain the flaxseeds (they will have a gelatinous texture), but do not rinse. Add the mixed seeds to the flaxseeds, then add the salt and spice (if using) and mix to combine.

Preheat the oven to 70°C (50°C fan-forced). Line two large baking trays with baking paper. Spread a very thin, even layer of the seed mixture over the prepared trays. Bake for 6 hours, flipping over halfway through to help the drying process. Remove from the oven and allow to cool completely on the trays. Cut into triangles or squares or break into pieces.

Place the tuna, lemon-infused olive oil and lemon zest in a bowl and mix to combine. Season with salt and pepper and sprinkle on the dill.

Serve the tuna with the crackers, mayonnaise or aioli, eggs, celery sticks, tomatoes and lemon slices.

## Note

You will have more flaxseed crackers than you need for this recipe. Store leftovers in an airtight container in the pantry for 2–4 weeks.

The older I get, the more I love and appreciate the versatility of the humble cabbage. If you think about all the delicious and healthy ways cabbage can be used, you soon realise it is pretty amazing: from gut-healing sauerkraut and spicy kimchi to cabbage rolls – so synonymous with Russian and Polish cooking – and buttery sautéed cabbage – the perfect accompaniment to roast pork. And let's not forget okonomiyaki (cabbage pancakes) from the streets of Japan and the luscious classic coleslaw found in southern USA. Coleslaw really is one of the best salads ever created, with all the fatty goodness that comes from smothering cabbage, veg and herbs in healthy aioli.

# COLESLAW

**SERVES 6**

1 carrot, grated
¼ red onion, thinly sliced
¼ savoy cabbage, finely shredded
¼ red cabbage, finely shredded
sea salt and freshly ground
    black pepper
1 handful of dill fronds, roughly
    chopped
1 handful of flat-leaf parsley leaves,
    roughly chopped
2 teaspoons finely grated lemon zest

**Dressing**
juice of 1 lemon
250 g (1 cup) Aioli (page 168) or
    Mayonnaise (page 174)

Place the carrot, onion and shredded cabbages in a large bowl. Set aside while you make the dressing.

To make the dressing, combine the lemon juice and aioli or mayonnaise in a bowl and mix well.

When ready to serve, season the vegetables with salt and pepper and add the herbs, lemon zest and dressing. Toss well and serve or portion into lunch containers.

We have seen many interpretations of classic dishes over the last decade or two from inventive chefs and home cooks looking for new ways to create their favourite dishes using seasonal produce. For some people, chickpeas can cause havoc in the gut, so in this recipe we substitute the chickpeas found in classic hummus with something gentler and more nurturing to the digestive system. You can replace the sweet potato with beetroot, pumpkin, avocado, parsnip, carrot, eggplant, mushrooms or artichokes.

# SWEET POTATO HUMMUS

## SERVES 4

3 sweet potatoes (about 240 g each)
3 tablespoons extra-virgin olive oil, plus extra to serve
2 tablespoons hulled tahini
2 tablespoons lemon juice
1 garlic clove, finely grated (optional)
1 teaspoon ground cumin
pinch of cayenne pepper (optional)
sea salt and freshly ground black pepper

**To serve**
sesame seeds, toasted
Coconut Flour Tortillas (page 170)

Preheat the oven to 200°C (180°C fan-forced). Line a baking tray with baking paper.

Prick the sweet potatoes with a fork a few times, place on the prepared tray and roast for 50 minutes until tender. Set aside until cool enough to handle, then peel away the skin and discard. Use a potato masher to mash the sweet potatoes until very smooth.

Place the sweet potato mash, olive oil, tahini, lemon juice, garlic (if using), cumin and cayenne pepper (if using) in the bowl of a food processor and blend until smooth and creamy. Season with salt and pepper. If the hummus is too thick, mix in a little cold water.

Spoon the hummus into a serving dish, drizzle over a little extra olive oil, sprinkle on the toasted sesame seeds and a pinch of salt and pepper and serve with the tortillas.

If you ever want to make your kids feel like rock stars at school, pack some crispy pork rinds and make sure they have extra to share with their mates! I don't think I have ever met a kid who doesn't like pork crackling, so why not give them what they like, especially as it is so delicious and healthy. If you choose to eat pork, always make sure you buy free-range – this is non-negotiable in my opinion.

# CRISPY PORK CRACKLING

## SERVES 4

600 g pork rind, with at least 5 mm
   of fat, scored
2 tablespoons coconut oil or
   good-quality animal fat*, melted
2 ½ teaspoons sea salt

* See Glossary

Brush the pork rind evenly with the oil or fat, then rub with the salt and set aside at room temperature for 20 minutes.

Preheat the oven to 240°C (220°C fan-forced).

Place the pork rind on a wire rack in a roasting tin. Roast, rotating the tin halfway to prevent burning, for 40 minutes, or until the pork crackling is golden and crisp. Keep a close eye on it in the final stages of cooking, as the edges may start to burn after 30 minutes.

Cool for 5 minutes, then cut into bite-sized pieces with kitchen scissors. The crackling is best eaten the same day, but will keep in an airtight container in the fridge for up to 2 days.

### Note
Reserve the leftover fat from the roasting tin and use it for cooking. Store the fat in an airtight container in the fridge for up to 2 weeks.

These vegetable crisps are a whole lot of fun. You could simply make with one type of vegetable, which would be perfectly delicious or, if you want to go the whole hog, you could do a variety, as we have done here. I guarantee they won't last long though, so make sure you make enough to go around.

# VEGETABLE CRISPS

## SERVES 4–6

500 ml (2 cups) coconut oil or
   good-quality animal fat*
1 sweet potato (about 240 g),
   thinly sliced with a mandoline
   or sharp knife
1 large parsnip (about 280 g),
   thinly sliced with a mandoline
   or sharp knife
sea salt
½ x quantity Kale Chips (page 173)

### Beetroot chips

2 beetroot
2 tablespoons coconut oil, melted
sea salt

* See Glossary

Preheat the oven to 140°C (120°C fan-forced). Line three or four large baking trays with baking paper.

To make the beetroot chips, peel the beetroot (wearing gloves to avoid staining your hands) and, using a mandoline, cut into 2 mm thick slices. If you don't have a mandoline, simply slice thinly with a sharp knife. Place the beetroot slices in a large bowl and, still wearing gloves, gently toss with the oil and season with salt. Arrange a single layer of beetroot slices on the trays and bake for 30 minutes. Rotate the trays and cook for a further 20 minutes until the beetroot is crisp at the edges, keeping a close eye on them to prevent burning. (The beetroot chips may need a few minutes longer, but they will crisp up as they cool.) Remove from the oven. Store in an airtight container in the pantry for up to 2 weeks.

Melt the oil or fat in a large saucepan over medium–high heat until the temperature reaches about 160°C. (To test, drop a sweet potato or parsnip slice into the hot oil; if it starts bubbling straight away, it is ready.) Fry the sliced sweet potato and parsnip separately in batches for 2–3½ minutes until just starting to colour. Remove from the oil, drain on paper towel and season with salt. Repeat with the remaining sliced vegetables. Keep a close eye when cooking at all times, as the crisps can burn very quickly. Store in an airtight container in the pantry for up to 3 days.

To serve, gently mix the kale and beetroot chips with the crisp sweet potato and parsnip.

### Tip

The oil or fat used for deep-frying can be re-used for deep-frying or cooking. Store it in a sealed container in the fridge for up to 2 weeks.

I enjoy a green juice from time to time. It is always organic, and I don't drink litres of it; usually just a glass every week or so. It's a good way to get an additional top-up of green goodness in your weekly diet. The goal with green juices, though, is to keep them as low-sugar as possible, so stick to a higher ratio of veggies to sweet fruits so you're not just drinking a big glass of sugar.

# GREEN JUICE

**SERVES 1–2**

¼ lemon
5 cm piece of ginger
½ bunch of silverbeet leaves (about 250 g), stems trimmed (you can also use kale or English spinach)
1–2 granny smith apples, cored
1 handful of mint leaves and stalks
1 handful of flat-leaf parsley leaves and stalks
1 Lebanese cucumber
ice cubes

Peel the lemon and ginger and chop into pieces.

Push all the ingredients, except the ice, through a juicer. Stir well.

To serve, place the ice cubes in one or two tall glasses or drink bottles and pour in the green juice.

Obviously, the optimum beverage for rehydration for our species is the best and purest water available. And water should make up the largest percentage of our daily fluid intake. That said, it is great from time to time to have drinks that contain other nutritional benefits. This is a healthy fat smoothie that will keep both kids and adults satisfied for long periods of time between meals. There is some wonderful carob grown in Australia, so you may like to swap the cacao out for carob. I would avoid having any cacao or caffeine after lunchtime to make sure you and your family get a good night's sleep.

# KETOGENIC CHOC-BERRY SMOOTHIE

## SERVES 2

400 ml coconut cream
100 ml coconut water
80 g fresh or frozen mixed berries,
    plus extra to serve
6 mint leaves
1 egg
1 tablespoon sunflower seeds
1 tablespoon pumpkin seeds
1 tablespoon chia seeds
3 tablespoons cacao or
    carob powder
1 tablespoon grass-fed
    collagen powder*

* See Glossary

Place all the ingredients in a blender and blend until smooth. Serve in a tall milkshake glass or, if you're on the go, in a bottle. Finish with some extra berries, if you like.

### Notes

If you prefer a little more sweetness, add stevia to taste.

This smoothie can be made in advance, frozen and then popped in your lunch box to thaw. Just give it a good shake before drinking.

PALEO WRAPS
COCONUT WRAPS
SUNFLOWER SEED CRACKERS
NUT-FREE PALEO BREAD
CAULIFLOWER ROLLS
CAULIFLOWER AND BACON TOAST
ENGLISH MUFFINS

These wraps are so simple to make and will soon become a family favourite.
Use them to whip up super-easy lunches for your household.

# PALEO WRAPS

## MAKES 10

4 eggs
40 g (¼ cup) sesame seeds, ground
   into a fine powder (use a spice
   grinder or mortar and pestle)
½ teaspoon sea salt
½ teaspoon garlic powder
60 g (½ cup) tapioca flour*
2½ tablespoons coconut oil or
   good-quality animal fat*

* See Glossary

Whisk the eggs, 2 tablespoons of water, the ground sesame seeds and the salt, garlic powder and tapioca flour together in a large bowl.

Melt 1 teaspoon of oil or fat in a 20 cm frying pan over medium heat and swirl around to coat the base of the pan. Pour in about 60 ml (¼ cup) of batter and tilt and swirl the pan to spread the batter into a thin round. Cook for about 1–1½ minutes until lightly golden brown on the underside. Flip and cook on the other side for 30 seconds, or until lightly golden. Set aside on a plate. Repeat with the remaining oil or fat and batter.

We enjoy making these and serving them as enchiladas or soft tacos for our favourite Mexican meals. If you like, make your coconut wraps a day ahead, then fill them on the day you are serving – they will be perfect. You will love how good these taste.

# COCONUT WRAPS

## MAKES 8

6 eggs
200 ml coconut milk
3 tablespoons coconut oil, melted
3 tablespoons coconut flour
3 tablespoons tapioca flour*
½ teaspoon sea salt
¼ teaspoon ground turmeric
  or curry powder

* See Glossary

Place the eggs, coconut milk, 1 tablespoon of coconut oil and 2 tablespoons of water in a bowl and whisk until smooth. Add the dry ingredients and whisk well to combine. To allow the dry ingredients to absorb the liquid, stand for 5–10 minutes. The batter is ready when it coats the back of a spoon.

Heat 1 teaspoon of the remaining oil in a frying pan over medium–high heat.

Give the batter a good mix, then pour about 80 ml (⅓ cup) of batter into the pan. Tilt and swirl the pan to spread the batter over the base and form a round about 20 cm in diameter. Cook for 1–2 minutes until golden brown on the underside. Flip and cook on the other side for about 30 seconds until lightly golden. Transfer to a plate and keep warm. Repeat until you have eight wraps.

You are going to love making these crackers, as they are just so easy.
They make the perfect light lunch or snack topped with your favourite dip or pâté.

# SUNFLOWER SEED CRACKERS

## MAKES ABOUT 20

130 g sunflower seeds
70 g tapioca flour*, plus extra
    for dusting
2 tablespoons white or
    black chia seeds
½ teaspoon fine sea salt
¼ teaspoon baking powder
2 tablespoons filtered water
2 tablespoons apple cider vinegar
extra-virgin olive oil, for brushing
flaky sea salt, for sprinkling

* See Glossary

Preheat the oven to 180°C (160°C fan-forced).

Combine the sunflower seeds, tapioca flour, chia seeds, fine sea salt and baking powder in the bowl of a high-speed blender or food processor and process to a fine powder. Add the water and vinegar and continue to process until the dough comes together to form a sticky paste.

Transfer the dough to a work surface dusted with tapioca flour. Roll into a ball, place on a large sheet of baking paper and press down to flatten into a disc. Allow to rest for 10 minutes. Place another large sheet of baking paper over the flattened dough and, using a rolling pin, roll out to a thickness of 2 mm. Peel away the top sheet of paper and discard.

Using a pizza cutter or sharp knife, cut the dough into rectangles about 5 cm x 8 cm. Transfer the dough shapes and the baking paper to a baking tray. Brush the shapes with a light coating of olive oil and sprinkle with the flaky salt. Bake, turning the tray halfway through, for 18–20 minutes until golden. Allow to cool completely before removing from the tray and serving. The crackers can be stored in an airtight container in the pantry for up to 1 week.

Many people think that when they go paleo, they need to eliminate bread from their diet altogether. This couldn't be further from the truth, and making your own healthy gluten-free bread doesn't take long. This bread recipe is nut free, too, so you can pack some for the kids' lunches.

# NUT-FREE PALEO BREAD

## ROUND ROLLS

### MAKES 6

70 g (1 cup) psyllium husks*
70 g (½ cup) coconut flour, plus extra
    for dusting
3 tablespoons chia seeds
3 tablespoons flaxseeds
30 g (¼ cup) pumpkin seeds, plus
    80 g extra, for sprinkling (optional)
3 tablespoons sesame seeds
30 g (¼ cup) sunflower seeds
1 tablespoon coconut sugar or honey
2 ½ teaspoons baking powder
1 ½ teaspoons sea salt
1 tablespoon apple cider vinegar
3 eggs
2 tablespoons coconut oil, melted

* See Glossary

Preheat the oven to 180°C (160°C fan-forced). Line a baking tray with baking paper.

Place the psyllium husks, coconut flour, chia seeds, flaxseeds, pumpkin seeds, sesame seeds and sunflower seeds in the bowl of a food processor and whiz for a few seconds until the seeds are finely chopped.

Transfer the flour mixture to a large bowl, then mix in the coconut sugar or honey, the baking powder and salt. In another bowl, combine the vinegar, 450 ml of water and the eggs and whisk until smooth. Add the coconut oil and the egg mixture to the dry ingredients and mix well to form a wet dough. Allow to stand for 2 minutes.

Knead the dough on a lightly floured work surface for 1 minute.

Divide the dough into six portions and roll into balls. Place the dough balls on the prepared tray, allowing room for spreading. Sprinkle with the extra pumpkin seeds if you like. Bake in the oven for 1 hour, rotating the tray halfway through so the rolls cook evenly. To check if they are cooked, tap the base of a roll. If it sounds hollow, the rolls are ready. If they seem to be very heavy and dense, they need to cook for a little longer.

## LONG ROLLS

### MAKES 6

Follow the steps above for preparing and kneading the dough. Divide the dough into six portions and roll into 12 cm long log shapes. Place on the prepared tray, allowing room for spreading, and bake in the oven for 1 hour, rotating the tray halfway through so the rolls cook evenly. To check if they are cooked, tap the base of a roll. If it sounds hollow, the rolls are ready. If they seem to be very heavy and dense, they need to cook for a little longer. Dust with a little coconut flour, if desired.

## BAGUETTES
### MAKES 2

Follow the steps on the previous page for preparing and kneading the dough. Divide the dough into two portions and roll into 30–35 cm long log shapes. Place the dough portions on the prepared tray, allowing room for spreading. Cut four or five 1 cm deep diagonal slits across the top of each baguette. This is mainly decorative, so if you like you can skip this step. Bake in the oven for 1 hour, rotating the tray halfway through so the baguettes cook evenly. To check if they are cooked, tap the base of a baguette. If it sounds hollow, they are ready. If they seem to be very heavy and dense, cook for a little longer.

## LOAF
### MAKES 1 (YOU GET 10–12 SLICES FROM 1 LOAF)

Grease a 20 cm x 10 cm loaf tin and line the base and sides with baking paper. Follow the steps on the previous page for preparing and kneading the dough, then roll the dough into one big ball. Place the dough in the prepared loaf tin and pat down. Bake in the oven for 1½ hours, rotating the tin halfway through so the loaf cooks evenly. To check if it is cooked, turn out the loaf and tap the base. If it sounds hollow, it's ready. If the loaf seems to be very heavy and dense, return to the tin and cook for a little longer.

Right: Long rolls used for Paleo Hot Dogs, page 142

Serve these buns with your favourite fillings, such as leg ham, sliced tomato, fresh basil and homemade mayonnaise.

# CAULIFLOWER ROLLS

## MAKES 10

800 g cauliflower florets
3 tablespoons tapioca flour*,
   plus extra for dusting
35 g (¼ cup) coconut flour
2 teaspoons baking powder
½ teaspoon garlic powder
1¼ teaspoons fine sea salt
3 eggs, beaten
1 teaspoon apple cider vinegar
1 tablespoon sesame seeds
1 tablespoon poppy seeds

* See Glossary

Preheat the oven to 180°C (160°C fan-forced). Line a baking tray with baking paper.

Place the cauliflower in the bowl of a food processor and process to very fine grains.

Combine the flours, baking powder, garlic powder and salt in a bowl and mix well. Add the cauliflower rice, eggs and vinegar, then, using your hands, knead until the mixture comes together to form a ball. The dough will be wet and sticky.

Divide the dough into ten portions and shape them into rough balls with your hands. Place the dough balls on the prepared tray, allowing room for spreading. Sprinkle on the sesame seeds and poppy seeds and bake for 1 hour, or until golden and a skewer inserted in the centre of a roll comes out clean. (You need to do the skewer test as these rolls are more dense than regular bread rolls and won't sound hollow when you tap them.) Transfer the rolls to a wire rack to cool.

Store the rolls in the fridge for up to 5 days or in the freezer for up to 3 months.

These fun little cauliflower toasts make a welcome addition to lunch boxes. Delicious cold or hot, make a big batch and serve with fried eggs and greens, or top with bacon or snags, or place under some grilled salmon or steak and add a dollop of delicious aioli.

# CAULIFLOWER AND BACON TOAST

## SERVES 4

¼ head of cauliflower (about 350 g),
   chopped into small pieces
2 ½ tablespoons coconut oil
sea salt and freshly ground
   black pepper
2 rindless bacon rashers
   (about 120 g), finely diced
2 eggs

**To serve**
lemon wedges
fried eggs
sliced avocado

Preheat the oven to 180°C (160°C fan-forced). Line a large baking tray with baking paper.

Place the cauliflower in the bowl of a food processor and process to fine crumbs.

Melt 1 tablespoon of the coconut oil in a large frying pan over medium heat. Add the cauliflower crumbs and cook for 4–6 minutes until softened. Season with salt and pepper, transfer to a large bowl and allow to cool.

Wipe the pan clean, add 2 teaspoons of the oil and fry the bacon over medium–high heat for 3–4 minutes until lightly golden. Allow to cool.

Add the cooled bacon to the cauliflower, add the eggs and mix to combine. Season with salt and pepper. Spoon 2 tablespoons of the cauliflower mixture onto the prepared tray and gently spread out to form a patty approximately 8 cm in diameter. Repeat, allowing 2 cm space between each patty, until all the mixture is used and you have four patties in total. Bake for 10 minutes, or until firm. Allow to cool.

Heat the remaining oil in a frying pan over medium–high heat. Cook the patties for 1–1 ½ minutes on each side until golden. Serve immediately with some lemon wedges, fried eggs and avocado.

These are a fun bread alternative to whip up and enjoy topped with eggs, snags, avocado or whatever else you love to use English muffins for. Or try this: drizzle some duck fat over the top of your muffins and simply grill until golden, then dip into your soup or braised dish. Yum!

# ENGLISH MUFFINS

## MAKES 10

6 eggs
100 ml coconut milk
80 ml (⅓ cup) coconut oil, melted,
   plus extra for greasing
1 teaspoon honey
35 g (¼ cup) coconut flour
80 g tapioca flour*
2 teaspoons baking powder
1 teaspoon sea salt

* See Glossary

Preheat the oven to 180°C (160°C fan-forced). Line a baking tray with baking paper and grease ten egg rings with oil.

In a bowl, whisk the eggs for 2 minutes, or until frothy. Mix in the coconut milk, oil and honey.

In another bowl, combine the coconut flour, tapioca flour, baking powder and salt. Add the egg mixture to the dry ingredients and mix until smooth. The consistency should be like pancake batter.

Place the egg rings on the prepared tray and, working quickly, pour 60 ml (¼ cup) of batter into each ring. Bake in the oven for 16–18 minutes until pale golden and cooked through. Place on a wire rack to cool.

SALAMI AND OLIVE MUFFINS

SPINACH AND MUSHROOM MUFFINS

CURRIED EGG MUFFINS

MONICA AND JACINTA'S FISH MUFFINS

WILD SALMON MUFFINS

BUTTER CHICKEN MUFFINS

PEKING DUCK MUFFINS WITH HOISIN SAUCE

BARBECUE PORK MUFFINS

MIDDLE EASTERN LAMB MUFFINS

GREEK-STYLE LAMB MUFFINS

SUPER-SIMPLE MEATY MUFFINS

BOLOGNESE MUFFINS WITH PESTO ZUCCHINI NOODLES

MEXICAN MINCE MUFFINS

There is a lot of talk about whether processed meats such as ham, salami and bacon are indeed healthy foods. My take on it is, if the pigs are healthy and have been fed a wholesome diet and raised in good conditions, and the curing process has been done in a traditional way (using good-quality salt), then, yes, by all means include some processed meat in your diet. If you don't have access to top-quality salami for this recipe, use roast chicken or pork or go vegetarian.

# SALAMI AND OLIVE MUFFINS

## MAKES 12

10 eggs
sea salt and freshly ground
   black pepper
12 large slices of salami
24 pitted kalamata olives or olives of
   your choice
24 Semi-dried Tomatoes (page 178)
24 basil leaves, torn

Preheat the oven to 180°C (160° fan-forced). Grease a 12-hole standard muffin tin.

Crack the eggs into a large bowl and lightly whisk. Season with salt and pepper.

Line each muffin hole with a slice of salami, covering the base and side completely. Evenly divide the olives, semi-dried tomatoes and basil among the holes, then spoon in the egg mixture until level with the rim. Bake for 15 minutes, or until the muffins have risen and a skewer inserted in the centre of a muffin comes out clean and dry. Allow the muffins to cool in the tin for 2 minutes before turning out. Serve the muffins while still warm or chill and use for school lunches. Store in an airtight container in the fridge for up to 2 days.

These cute and delicious muffins are a great way to get veggies into your kids' diets. They take no time at all and the recipe makes heaps. If your kids aren't keen on mushrooms, swap them with another veggie they love, such as roasted pumpkin or sweet potato. We like to serve these with a green herb sauce, lettuce, sauerkraut and olives.

# SPINACH AND MUSHROOM MUFFINS

## MAKES 12

2 tablespoons coconut oil or good-quality animal fat*, plus extra for greasing
1 leek, white part only, or onion, chopped
250 g cup or field mushrooms or mushrooms of your choice, halved
2 garlic cloves, chopped
120 g baby spinach leaves
6 eggs
sea salt and freshly ground black pepper
6 cherry tomatoes, halved

## To serve
150 g Nut-free Basil and Parsley Pesto (see page 82)
lettuce leaves (such as butter lettuce, baby cos, iceberg, rocket)
green or black olives
Sauerkraut (page 177)

* See Glossary

Preheat the oven to 180°C (160°C fan-forced). Grease a 12-hole standard muffin tin with oil or fat.

Heat the oil or fat in a frying pan over medium heat. Add the leek or onion and sauté for 5 minutes, or until softened. Next, add the mushrooms and sauté for 5 minutes, or until softened, then add the garlic and cook for a further 1 minute. Remove from the heat and allow to cool.

Place the cooked leek/onion and mushroom mixture in the bowl of a food processor. Add the spinach and pulse a couple of times until coarsely chopped. Set aside.

Crack the eggs into a large bowl and whisk until smooth. Add the mushroom and spinach mixture and mix until well combined. Season with salt and pepper.

Spoon the mixture evenly into each hole of the prepared muffin tin until level with the rim, then top with a cherry tomato half. Bake for 15–20 minutes until the muffins have risen and a skewer inserted in the centre of a muffin comes out clean. Allow the muffins to cool in the tin for 2 minutes before turning out onto a wire rack to cool completely.

Serve the muffins with some pesto spooned over the top and with a side of lettuce, olives and sauerkraut. The muffins can be stored in an airtight container in the fridge for up to 5 days.

Curry and egg work so well together that I just had to include this wonderful flavour combo somewhere in this book. The joy of making these muffins is that everyone loves them; they'll be happy to eat them at any time of the day and they are perfect for school and work lunches. I have kept these vegetarian, but you can easily add some ham, bacon, cooked chicken or prawns.

# CURRIED EGG MUFFINS

## MAKES 12

2 tablespoons coconut oil or
   good-quality animal fat*,
   plus extra for greasing
1 onion, chopped
2 garlic cloves, finely chopped
1 tablespoon chopped coriander
   leaves or curly or flat-leaf
   parsley leaves
8 eggs
3 teaspoons curry powder
150 g cauliflower florets,
   finely chopped
1 teaspoon fine sea salt
freshly ground black pepper

## Curried mayonnaise
200 g Mayonnaise (page 174)
1 teaspoon curry powder

## To serve
poppy seeds
1 small handful of Crispy Curry
   Leaves (page 172)
2 spring onions, chopped
Vegetable Crisps (we used
   parsnip, see page 34)
Kale Chips (page 173)
black or green grapes

* See Glossary

To make the curried mayonnaise, combine the mayo and curry powder in a bowl and mix well. Set aside until needed.

Preheat the oven to 200°C (180°C fan-forced). Line a 12-hole standard muffin tin with paper cases.

Heat the oil or fat in a frying pan over medium heat. Add the onion and sauté for 5 minutes, or until softened and translucent. Add the garlic and cook for a further 1 minute. Remove from the heat, mix through the coriander or parsley and allow to cool.

Crack the eggs into a large bowl, add the curry powder and whisk until smooth, then stir in the cauliflower. Season with salt and pepper.

Spoon the onion mixture evenly into each hole of the prepared muffin tin, then pour in the egg mixture until level with the rim. Bake for 15 minutes, or until the muffins have risen and a skewer inserted in the centre of a muffin comes out clean and dry. Allow the muffins to cool in the tin for 2 minutes before turning out onto a wire rack. Sprinkle over the poppy seeds, crispy curry leaves and spring onion and serve while still warm or cold with the parsnip crisps, kale chips, grapes and curried mayonnaise on the side. Store the muffins in an airtight container in the fridge for up to 2 days.

Monica and her twin sister, Jacinta, are brilliant chefs and dear friends, who have been working alongside me for the last 12 years. I trust them with my life and the lives of my children. From time to time the girls look after my daughters and have them for sleepovers. On these occasions, Monica and Jacinta make their famous fish muffins, which go down a treat! I always ask for a batch so we can pack them into lunch boxes during the week. Thanks ladies, I am forever indebted to you both, xo.

# MONICA AND JACINTA'S FISH MUFFINS

## MAKES 12

1 large zucchini (about 240 g), grated
2 carrots (about 200 g), grated
1½ teaspoons fine sea salt
coconut oil or good-quality
    animal fat*, for greasing
4 eggs, beaten
¼ teaspoon bicarbonate of soda
280 g tuna, salmon, mackerel or
    sardines in brine or spring water*,
    drained
2 tablespoons chopped curly or
    flat-leaf parsley leaves
2 teaspoons coconut flour
zest of ½ lemon
freshly ground black pepper

**Quick tartare sauce**
200 g Mayonnaise (page 174)
1 tablespoon salted capers, rinsed well,
    patted dry and chopped

**To serve**
lemon cheeks
1 baby cos lettuce, leaves separated

* See Glossary

Combine the zucchini and carrot in a colander. Sprinkle with the salt and mix through. Leave the vegetables to release moisture for 15 minutes, then squeeze out all the liquid from the zucchini and carrot with your hands. You can also wrap the vegetables in a clean tea towel and squeeze the liquid out that way.

Preheat the oven to 200°C (180°C fan-forced). Grease a 12-hole standard muffin tin with oil or fat.

Place the eggs and bicarbonate of soda in a large bowl and whisk to combine. Add the zucchini and carrot, fish, parsley, coconut flour and lemon zest and season with some pepper. Mix until well incorporated. Spoon the mixture evenly into the holes of the prepared muffin tin. Bake for 25 minutes, or until the muffins are firm and cooked through. Allow the muffins to cool in the tin for 2 minutes before turning out onto a wire rack to cool completely.

Meanwhile, to make the quick tartare sauce, place the mayonnaise and capers in a small bowl and mix to combine. Set aside until needed.

Serve the muffins with some tartare sauce and the lemon cheeks and cos lettuce leaves on the side.

I think many kids miss out on good-quality seafood. We always make sure our girls eat fish and seafood a few times a week, both at home and at school. This is a super-easy recipe that any kid (or adult) would love to take to school (or work). It also makes a perfect easy dinner and a great brekkie to grab and go. I have teamed these salmon muffins with lettuce, celery and mayo, but feel free to add any sauce and your family's favourite salad or veg.

# WILD SALMON MUFFINS

## MAKES 12

1 tablespoon coconut oil or
   good-quality animal fat*,
   plus extra for greasing
½ red onion, finely chopped
½ red capsicum, deseeded and
   finely chopped
5 eggs, lightly beaten
415 g wild pink or red salmon*
   in olive oil or brine, drained
1 tablespoon coconut flour
2 tablespoons finely chopped curly
   or flat-leaf parsley leaves
1 handful of baby spinach leaves,
   chopped
2 teaspoons Dijon mustard
½ teaspoon sea salt
freshly ground black pepper

### To serve
½ iceberg lettuce, cut into wedges
2 celery stalks, cut into 6 cm batons
1 lemon, cut into slices
150 g Mayonnaise (page 174)

* See Glossary

Preheat the oven to 200°C (180°C fan-forced). Grease 12 star-shaped silicone moulds or a 12-hole standard muffin tin with oil or fat.

Heat the oil or fat in a frying pan over medium heat. Add the onion and capsicum and fry for 5 minutes, or until softened and starting to colour slightly. Remove from the heat and allow to cool.

In a bowl, combine the eggs, salmon, coconut flour, parsley, spinach, mustard and the cooked onion and capsicum and mix well with your hands or a wooden spoon. Season with salt and pepper. Spoon the mixture evenly into the prepared moulds or muffin tin. Bake for 20 minutes, or until the muffins are firm and cooked through. Allow the muffins to cool in the moulds or tin for 2 minutes before turning out onto a wire rack to cool completely.

Serve the muffins (on wooden skewers, if desired) with the lettuce wedges, celery sticks, lemon slices and mayonnaise on the side.

My paleo butter chicken has become a dinner-time staple for many families. This recipe came about because I wanted to incorporate all that deliciousness into a muffin.

# BUTTER CHICKEN MUFFINS

## MAKES 12

2 tablespoons coconut oil or
    good-quality animal fat*, melted,
    plus extra for greasing
1½ onions, chopped
3 garlic cloves, finely chopped
600 g chicken mince
260 ml coconut cream
1 egg, beaten
1½ teaspoons sea salt

### Butter chicken curry paste
1 tablespoon coconut oil, softened
2 teaspoons garam masala
1 teaspoon ground cardamom
1 teaspoon ground coriander
1 teaspoon ground ginger
1 teaspoon ground cumin
1 teaspoon sweet paprika
1–2 pinches of cayenne pepper
    (optional)
1 teaspoon ground turmeric
3 tablespoons tomato paste
1 tablespoon lemon juice

### Roasted cauliflower
½ head of cauliflower (about 600 g),
    broken into florets
2 tablespoons coconut oil, melted
freshly ground black pepper

### To serve
1 x quantity Raita (page 176)
1 small handful of coriander leaves
6 lime cheeks

* See Glossary

To make the butter chicken curry paste, blend all the ingredients together to form a wet paste.

Heat a non-stick frying pan over medium heat. Add the curry paste and cook, stirring frequently, for 2½–3 minutes, or until the paste pulls away from the pan and is fragrant. Allow to cool.

Preheat the oven to 200°C (180°C fan-forced). Lightly grease a 12-hole standard muffin tin.

Heat the oil or fat in a frying pan over medium heat. Add the onion and sauté for 5 minutes, or until translucent. Add the garlic and cook for 30 seconds to soften. Remove from the heat, set aside and allow to cool.

In a large bowl, combine the chicken mince with the coconut cream, eggs, curry paste and the cooled onion mixture and salt and mix well. Spoon evenly into each hole of the prepared muffin tin. Place the muffin tin on a baking tray (some liquid may drip from the tin during cooking) and bake for 15–20 minutes. Allow to rest in the tin for 5 minutes before turning out.

Meanwhile, to roast the cauliflower, blanch the cauliflower in boiling water for 2 minutes, or until just tender and slightly crunchy in the centre. Drain in a colander and set aside to steam dry. (You don't want any moisture left on the cauliflower as it won't roast properly.) Line a baking tray with baking paper. Drizzle the oil over the cauliflower and toss to coat. Scatter the cauliflower in a single layer over the prepared tray and season with salt and pepper. Roast for 15–20 minutes until golden and tender.

Serve the butter chicken muffins with the roasted cauliflower, raita, coriander leaves and lime.

One of my favourite rituals with my kids is to take them to a good Chinese restaurant to share roast duck with veggies on the side. Here, I wanted to replicate those amazing flavours and freshen things up a little with the addition of lettuce cups, cucumber, spring onion and carrot. If you can't find duck breast, use pork, turkey or chicken mince instead.

# PEKING DUCK MUFFINS WITH HOISIN SAUCE

## MAKES 12

coconut oil or good-quality
    animal fat*, for greasing
4 duck breasts, skin removed and
    rendered (see Rendered Animal
    Fat page 176)
2 garlic cloves, roughly chopped
2 teaspoons finely grated ginger
1 tablespoon finely chopped
    coriander leaves
1 tablespoon honey
2 tablespoons tamari or coconut aminos*
1 teaspoon Chinese five spice
2 eggs

### Hoisin sauce

juice of 1 orange
2 tablespoons hulled tahini
1 teaspoon grated garlic
1 tablespoon grated ginger
2 teaspoons apple cider vinegar
2 tablespoons honey
80 ml (⅓ cup) tamari or coconut aminos*
½ teaspoon Chinese five spice
1½ teaspoons sesame oil
½ teaspoon chilli flakes or chilli powder
2 teaspoons tomato paste

### To serve

black and white sesame seeds, toasted
1½ baby cos lettuces, leaves separated
1 carrot, cut into 6 cm strips
1 Lebanese cucumber, deseeded,
    cut into 6 cm strips
2 spring onions, cut into 6 cm strips

* See Glossary

To make the hoisin sauce, place all the ingredients in a saucepan. Add 80 ml (⅓ cup) of water and bring to a simmer over medium–low heat. Cook, stirring constantly, for 5 minutes. Allow to cool, then blend until smooth, adding more water if necessary. Store in an airtight container in the fridge for up to 1 week.

Preheat the oven to 180°C (160°C fan-forced) and lightly grease a 12-hole standard muffin tin with oil or fat.

Place the duck, garlic, ginger and coriander in the bowl of a food processor and pulse a few times until finely chopped. Add the honey, tamari or coconut aminos, the rendered duck fat, five spice and eggs and pulse a couple more times to combine. Spoon the mixture evenly into the holes of the prepared tin, then bake for 10–15 minutes, or until the muffins are cooked through. Cool slightly in the tin for 1 minute. The muffins may release a little bit of liquid, so drain well before you turn them out of the tin.

Using a pastry brush, brush a light coating of hoisin sauce over each muffin. Place the muffins in a shallow bowl, sprinkle with the sesame seeds and serve with the lettuce, carrot, cucumber, spring onion and remaining hoisin sauce on the side.

These pulled pork muffins with crispy crackling are incredibly indulgent. And, I have to say, they are delicious and will change the way you look at school and work lunches. They are so good I recommend you cook a double batch: serve with coleslaw for dinner and pack the leftovers in your lunch box the next day.

# BARBECUE PORK MUFFINS

## MAKES 12

3 tablespoons coconut oil or
    good-quality animal fat*, melted,
    plus extra for greasing
1 kg boned pork shoulder, skin
    removed, trimmed, rinsed and
    patted dry with paper towel
sea salt and freshly ground
    black pepper
3 tablespoons maple syrup
1 tablespoon garlic powder
½ teaspoon mustard powder
1 tablespoon onion powder
½ teaspoon freshly ground
    white pepper
125 ml (½ cup) Smoked Barbecue
    Sauce (page 178)
125 ml (½ cup) Worcestershire Sauce
    (page 180)
2 tablespoons finely chopped curly
    or flat-leaf parsley leaves
4 eggs, lightly beaten

### To serve
Coleslaw (page 29)
200 g Crispy Pork Crackling
    (page 32)
1 tablespoon finely snipped chives

* See Glossary

Preheat the oven to 170°C (150°C fan-forced). Lightly grease a roasting tin with oil or fat.

Cut the pork in half, then rub with 1 tablespoon of oil or fat. Sprinkle with salt and pepper. Heat the remaining oil or fat in a large frying pan over high heat. Add the pork halves and sear for 2 minutes on all sides until lightly browned. Transfer the pork, fat-side up, to the prepared tin.

Mix the maple syrup, garlic, mustard and onion powders, white pepper, sauces and 750 ml (3 cups) of water in a bowl. Pour over the pork, cover the tin with a lid (or use a slow cooker) and roast for 1 hour. Reduce the oven temperature to 110°C (90°C fan-forced) and continue roasting for 8–9 hours, or until the pork is very tender and easy to pull away from the bone. Remove the pork, reserving the liquid. Slice or shred the pork. Set aside. Strain the reserved liquid through a fine sieve into a saucepan and reduce by half over medium–high heat. Pour 250 ml (1 cup) of reduced liquid over the pulled pork and mix well. Allow to cool.

Place the remaining liquid over medium–high heat and boil until reduced to a thick sauce consistency. Set aside to cool.

Increase the oven temperature to 180°C (160°C fan-forced) and lightly grease a 12-hole standard muffin tin with oil or fat.

Add the parsley and egg to the cooled pulled pork and mix well to combine. Season with salt and pepper and spoon evenly into each hole of the prepared muffin tin. Bake for 15 minutes, then baste the muffin tops lightly with the reduced sauce. Return to the oven to bake for a further 15 minutes, or until the muffins are firm and golden. Cool in the tin for 10 minutes before turning out. Drizzle some of the remaining sauce over the muffins and serve with the coleslaw and pork crackling and a sprinkling of chives.

Lamb, goat, kangaroo and venison all pair beautifully with Middle Eastern flavours. Feel free to play around with these other meats if they're available. I have teamed these muffins with a spiced coconut yoghurt, but you could easily use tahini or mayonnaise if you prefer. Serve with cucumber and radish to finish it off.

# MIDDLE EASTERN LAMB MUFFINS

## MAKES 12

80 ml (⅓ cup) good-quality animal fat*, melted, plus extra for greasing
½ onion, chopped
3 garlic cloves, finely chopped
500 g lamb mince
1 roma or truss tomato, deseeded and finely diced
1 tablespoon pomegranate molasses*, plus extra to serve
2 eggs, beaten
1½ teaspoons fine sea salt

### Spice mix
35 g (⅓ cup) ground cumin
3 tablespoons dried mint
3 tablespoons dried oregano
2 tablespoons sweet paprika
2 tablespoons freshly ground black pepper
2 teaspoons hot paprika

### Mint and radish salad
1 large handful of watercress or rocket
1 handful of mint leaves
1 Lebanese cucumber, thinly sliced on a mandoline
3 radishes, thinly sliced on a mandoline
seeds from ½ pomegranate
2 tablespoons lemon juice
3 tablespoons extra-virgin olive oil, plus extra to serve

### To serve
2–3 pinches of sumac*
Coconut Yoghurt (page 171)

* See Glossary

To make the spice mix, place all the ingredients in an airtight container and shake to combine. Store in an airtight container in the pantry for up to 6 months.

Preheat the oven to 200°C (180°C fan-forced) and lightly grease a 9-hole giant (250 ml/1 cup) muffin tin with fat.

Heat 2 tablespoons of the fat in a frying pan over medium heat. Add the onion and sauté until softened and translucent. Add the garlic and cook for a further minute. Set aside.

In a large bowl, mix the lamb mince, cooked onion mixture, 2 tablespoons of spice mix, the tomato, pomegranate molasses, remaining fat and the eggs and salt until well incorporated. Spoon the mixture evenly into the prepared tin, then bake for 15–20 minutes, or until the muffins are cooked through. Cool slightly in the tin for 1 minute. The muffins may release a little bit of liquid, so drain well before you turn them out.

Meanwhile, to make the salad, place all the ingredients in a bowl and gently toss with your hands until coated with the lemon juice and olive oil. Season with salt.

Sprinkle the sumac and drizzle a little extra olive oil over the coconut yoghurt. Divide the muffins among serving plates or lunch containers and drizzle the extra pomegranate molasses over the top. Serve the muffins with the salad and spiced coconut yoghurt.

### Note
The spice mix in this recipe can be used as a rub for any kind of meat or to season vegetable dishes or stews.

Who doesn't love lamb and mint? Growing up, I remember having mint jelly on my roast lamb – with this delicious lunch-box treat I hope to recreate that memory for school kids everywhere. Use good-quality lamb mince to make a double batch of these super-yummy muffins, then enjoy for dinner — and lunch the next day.

# GREEK-STYLE LAMB MUFFINS

## MAKES 12

80 ml (⅓ cup) coconut oil or
   good-quality animal fat*,
   plus extra for greasing
1 red onion, finely chopped
3 garlic cloves, finely chopped
1 teaspoon ground cumin
¼ teaspoon chilli flakes (optional)
600 g lamb mince
1 tablespoon dried mint
2 tablespoons dried oregano
2 eggs, lightly beaten
sea salt and freshly ground
   black pepper

## To serve
salad of your choice
Mint Jelly (page 174)

* See Glossary

Preheat the oven to 180°C (160°C fan-forced) and lightly grease a 12-hole standard muffin tin with a little oil or fat.

Heat the oil or fat in a frying pan over medium heat. Add the onion and sauté for about 5 minutes until softened and translucent. Add the garlic and cook for a further minute, then add the cumin and chilli flakes (if using) and cook for 30 seconds, or until fragrant. Set aside.

In a large bowl, mix the lamb mince with the cooked onion mixture, dried herbs, eggs and some salt and pepper until well incorporated. Spoon the mixture evenly into the holes of the prepared tin, then bake for 15–20 minutes until the muffins are cooked through. Cool slightly for 1 minute. The muffins may release a little bit of liquid, so drain well before you turn them out of the tin. Serve the muffins with a salad of your choice and some mint jelly on the side.

There is nothing remotely hard about this recipe and there is no reason you can't cook up a big batch of meaty muffins on Sunday, enjoy them for lunch or dinner, then use the leftover muffins for lunches for the first couple of days of the school week. Simply presented in the lunch box with some fresh salad, a low-sugar tomato ketchup and some gherkins or olives, they'll go down an absolute treat.

# SUPER-SIMPLE MEATY MUFFINS

## MAKES 12

1 tablespoon coconut oil or
   good-quality animal fat*,
   plus extra for greasing
3 garlic cloves, finely chopped
1 onion, finely chopped
2 rindless bacon rashers,
   finely chopped
600 g beef mince
1 egg
80 g (½ cup) grated carrot
2 tablespoons chopped flat-leaf
   parsley leaves
1 teaspoon dried oregano
½ teaspoon ground cumin
1 ½ tablespoons tamari or
   coconut aminos*
pinch each of sea salt and freshly
   ground black pepper

### To serve
Tomato Ketchup (page 180)
2 tomatoes, sliced
6 gherkins, sliced
Mayonnaise (page 174) or
   Aioli (page 168)
2 baby cos lettuces,
   leaves separated

* See Glossary

Preheat the oven to 200°C (180°C fan-forced) and lightly grease a 12-hole standard muffin tin with oil or fat.

Heat the oil or fat in a frying pan. Add the garlic, onion and bacon and sauté, stirring occasionally, for 6 minutes, or until browned. Remove from the heat and set aside.

Combine the mince, egg, carrot, parsley, oregano, cumin and tamari or coconut aminos in a bowl. Add the onion mixture, season with salt and pepper and combine well.

Spoon the mixture evenly into the holes of the prepared muffin tin. Bake for 15 minutes, or until the meaty muffins are perfectly juicy.

Spoon some tomato ketchup over each muffin, then add a slice of tomato, some gherkin and a dollop of mayo or aioli and serve with the cos leaves.

When you have leftover bolognese, these muffins make the perfect school
or work lunch or after-school snack.

# BOLOGNESE MUFFINS
# WITH PESTO ZUCCHINI NOODLES

## MAKES 24

2 tablespoons coconut oil or
    good-quality animal fat*,
    plus extra for greasing
1 onion, finely chopped
80 g (½ cup) finely diced carrot
60 g finely diced celery
3 garlic cloves, finely chopped
450 g beef mince
2 tablespoons finely chopped
    flat-leaf parsley leaves
1 teaspoon dried oregano
1 egg
pumpkin seeds, toasted, to serve

### Tomato sauce

2 tablespoons coconut oil or
    good-quality animal fat*
1 onion, chopped
4 garlic cloves, finely chopped
2 tablespoons tomato paste
80 ml (⅓ cup) dry white wine
400 g tomato passata
200 ml Chicken Bone Broth (page 170)
1 handful of basil leaves, torn
sea salt and freshly ground
    black pepper

### Nut-free basil and parsley pesto

4 large handfuls of basil leaves,
    plus extra to serve
4 roasted garlic cloves
2 tablespoons pumpkin seeds, toasted
1–2 tablespoons lemon juice
130 ml extra-virgin olive oil, to taste

### Zucchini noodles

800 g zucchini (about 4)
1 tablespoon coconut oil

* See Glossary

To make the tomato sauce, heat the oil or fat in a saucepan
over medium heat, add the onion and cook for 5 minutes,
or until softened and translucent. Add the garlic and
tomato paste and sauté for 1 minute, or until the onion
and garlic are starting to caramelise. Pour in the wine and
bring to the boil. Stir in the tomato passata and broth and
simmer for 30 minutes. Add the basil and simmer for a
further 5 minutes. Season with salt and pepper.

Meanwhile, preheat the oven to 180°C (160°C fan-forced)
and lightly grease a 24-hole mini muffin tin with oil or fat.

Heat the oil or fat in a frying pan over medium heat. Add the
onion, carrot and celery and cook for 5 minutes, or until the
vegetables have softened. Add the garlic and cook for a
further 1 minute, or until fragrant. Set aside.

In a large bowl, mix the beef mince with the cooked onion
mixture, the parsley, oregano, egg, 1½ teaspoons of salt
and 1 teaspoon of pepper until well incorporated.

Spoon the meat mixture evenly into each hole of the
prepared muffin tin. Bake for 7–8 minutes until the muffins
are cooked through. Cool in the tin for 1 minute. The
muffins may release a little bit of liquid, so drain well and
reserve the liquid before you turn them out of the tin.

Mix the reserved liquid through the tomato sauce, then
gently stir in the muffins.

To make the pesto, place all the ingredients in a mortar or
food processor and combine to form a thick, coarse paste.
Taste and season with salt and pepper.

To make the noodles, first spiralise the zucchini. Heat the
coconut oil in a frying pan over medium–high heat. Add the
zucchini noodles and sauté for 1–1½ minutes until slightly
soft. Season with salt and pepper, add the pesto and toss well.
Continue to cook for 30 seconds, or until heated through.

Divide the muffins and sauce between serving plates or
lunch containers, sprinkle over the pumpkin seeds and
serve with the pesto zucchini noodles and basil leaves.

Mexican mince, one of the easiest and tastiest elements to combine with fresh and flavourful ingredients, is the hero in these super-easy muffins. To leave the whole family feeling satisfied, serve with your favourite taco or nacho toppings, such as guacamole, tomato salsa and coriander leaves. I do love sweet potato crisps too, and, if you are so inclined, some coconut sour cream and a little jalapeno chilli are perfect additions.

# MEXICAN MINCE MUFFINS

## MAKES 12

2 tablespoons coconut oil or
    good-quality animal fat*,
    plus extra for greasing
1 onion, finely chopped
4 garlic cloves, finely chopped
1 red capsicum, deseeded and
    finely chopped
2 long red chillies, deseeded and
    finely chopped (optional)
2 teaspoons smoked paprika
2 teaspoons ground cumin
1½ teaspoons ground coriander
3 tablespoons tomato paste
500 g beef mince
2 eggs
2 tablespoons chopped coriander leaves
3 tablespoons Chicken or Beef Bone
    Broth (page 170 or 168) or water
1½ teaspoons fine sea salt
½ teaspoon finely ground black pepper

### Cherry tomato salad

250 g cherry tomatoes, quartered
2 tablespoons chopped red onion
1 tablespoon finely chopped
    coriander leaves
2 tablespoons lime juice
3 tablespoons extra-virgin olive oil

### To serve

6 iceberg lettuce leaves
Guacamole (page 173)
Vegetable Crisps (we used sweet
    potato, see page 34)
coriander sprigs
lime cheeks

* See Glossary

Preheat the oven to 180°C (160°C fan-forced). Lightly grease a 12-hole standard muffin tin with oil or fat.

Heat the oil or fat in a frying pan over medium heat. Add the onion and sauté until softened and translucent. Add the garlic, capsicum and chilli (if using) and cook for a further 3 minutes, or until the capsicum is softened. Add the spices and tomato paste and cook for 1 minute, or until fragrant. Remove from the heat and allow to cool.

In a large bowl, mix the beef mince, cooked onion and capsicum mixture, eggs, coriander leaves, bone broth and salt and pepper until well incorporated. Spoon the mixture evenly into each hole of the prepared tin, then bake for 18–20 minutes until the muffins are cooked through. Cool slightly in the tin for 1 minute. The muffins may release a little bit of liquid, so drain well before you turn them out of the tin.

To make the tomato salad, combine all the ingredients in a bowl and gently mix. Season with salt and pepper.

Place a lettuce leaf on each serving plate or in each lunch container, then top with two muffins. Serve with the tomato salad, guacamole, sweet potato crisps, coriander sprigs and lime cheeks.

CHICKEN, CARROT AND SWEET POTATO NORI ROLLS

AVOCADO AND SEAFOOD NORI ROLLS

SALMON AND BROCCOLI NORI ROLLS

CHICKEN LIVER PÂTÉ

FISH AND EGG SALAD LETTUCE CUPS

HAM AND SALAD WRAPS

BLT WITH TURKEY

CHICKEN AND AVOCADO ROLLS

SAUSAGE ROLL EGG WRAPS

MINESTRONE

CHICKEN AND PARSLEY BROTH

JOY'S CHICKEN AND VEGETABLE SOUP

CHICKEN CAESAR SALAD

SIMPLE NIÇOISE SALAD

ZUCCHINI NOODLES WITH CHICKEN AND PESTO

WILD SALMON CAKES

CHICKEN LARB MEATBALLS IN CABBAGE CUPS

BEEF AND THYME SAUSAGE ROLLS

CHILLI−LAMB SAUSAGE ROLLS

SAUSAGE, BACON AND EGG MUFFINS

ZUCCHINI AND ONION BHAJIS

CHICKEN NUGGETS

PALEO NACHOS

MEXICAN BEEF MINCE WITH AVO TACOS

AVOCADO BOWL WITH BLT, CHICKEN AND EGG

HONEY, GINGER AND SOY CHICKEN DRUMSTICKS

OKONOMIYAKI

PALEO HOT DOGS

My kids enjoy anything wrapped in a nori sheet. Here, we have teamed chicken —
you can use leftover roast or freshly cooked — with some sweet potato to help bind.
What I love about this recipe is the different combination of flavours you can play around
with, so you and your family will never get bored. You can make these the night before
and they will be great for the next day's lunch.

# CHICKEN, CARROT AND
# SWEET POTATO NORI ROLLS

## SERVES 4

230 g Sweet Potato Puree
   (page 179), cold
400 g (2 cups) Cauliflower Rice
   (page 169), cold
sea salt
4 toasted nori sheets*
2 teaspoons Mayonnaise (page 174),
   plus extra to serve
200 g cooked chicken thigh or
   breast, cut into strips
½ Lebanese cucumber, deseeded
   and cut into strips
½ carrot, cut into thin batons
tamari or coconut aminos*, to serve

* See Glossary

Place the sweet potato puree and cauliflower rice in a bowl and mix to combine. Season with salt.

Place a nori sheet, rough-side up, on a bench or bamboo sushi mat. Spread one-quarter of the cauliflower rice mixture onto half the nori sheet, working from the edge closest to you and spreading it out to the sides. Spread ½ teaspoon of the mayonnaise down the middle of the cauliflower rice, then layer on a quarter of the chicken, cucumber and carrot. Starting with the edge closest to you, tightly wrap up the roll. If the nori roll doesn't seal, brush a little water on the inside edge of the nori sheet, then continue to roll to seal. Repeat this process with the remaining nori sheets, cauliflower rice mixture, mayonnaise and fillings.

Trim the ends of each roll with a sharp knife, then cut into 2.5 cm rounds. Serve with the tamari or coconut aminos and the extra mayonnaise.

It is good to see that people are looking for healthier options when it comes to lunchtime meals. Making lunch at home with minimal fuss, using the most beautiful ingredients, is better for you and better than having to pay a fortune for it. This is a favourite in our home. Swap out the fish for cooked prawns or smoked eel, or, if you prefer, some roast pork or beef. Have a play around with different seasonal veggies, and for some added texture you can easily include broccoli rice. The kids will love these rolls in their school lunch boxes.

# AVOCADO AND SEAFOOD NORI ROLLS

## SERVES 4

1 avocado
2 teaspoons lemon juice
400 g (2 cups) Cauliflower Rice
  (page 169), cold
sea salt and freshly ground
  black pepper
185 g tuna, salmon, mackerel or
  sardines in olive oil or brine*,
  drained
80 g Mayonnaise (page 174),
  plus extra to serve
4 toasted nori sheets*
½ Lebanese cucumber, deseeded
  and cut lengthways into 1 cm
  thick sticks
2 teaspoons toasted sesame seeds
tamari or coconut aminos*, to serve

* See Glossary

Place the avocado and lemon juice in the bowl of a food processor and blend until smooth and creamy. Transfer to a bowl, add the cauliflower rice and mix to combine. Season with salt and pepper.

In another bowl, mix the fish with 2 tablespoons of the mayonnaise.

Place a nori sheet, rough-side up, on a bench or bamboo sushi mat. Spread one-quarter of the cauliflower rice mixture onto half the nori sheet, working from the edge closest to you and spreading it out to the sides. Layer on one-quarter of the fish mixture and cucumber and dollop on 2 teaspoons of the remaining mayonnaise. Starting with the edge closest to you, tightly wrap up the roll. If the nori roll doesn't seal, brush a little water on the inside edge of the nori sheet, then continue to roll to seal. Lightly brush the top of the nori roll with water, then sprinkle on ½ teaspoon of sesame seeds. (The light coating of water helps the sesame seeds to stick.) Repeat with the remaining nori, fillings and sesame seeds.

Trim the ends of each nori roll with a sharp knife, then cut into 2.5 cm rounds. Serve with the tamari or coconut aminos for dipping.

### Note
I don't recommend eating too much tuna, due to high levels of mercury. Some tuna from time to time is fine, but not every day.

If there is one way to get broccoli into a school lunch box, here it is. The broccoli rice nori roll is the best thing since sliced paleo bread and is coming to a sushi bar near you soon! Full of nutritious goodness, we have teamed nori with avocado, wild salmon and cucumber and added some sauerkraut on the side for good gut health. Feel free to replace the salmon with cooked prawns or chicken or whatever animal protein you love to eat.

# SALMON AND BROCCOLI NORI ROLLS

## SERVES 4

50 g Mayonnaise (page 174),
　　plus 1 tablespoon extra
450 g (2 cups) Broccoli Rice
　　(page 169), cold
sea salt and freshly ground
　　black pepper
4 toasted nori sheets*
150 g sashimi-grade salmon,
　　skin off, cut into 1 cm strips
1 Lebanese cucumber, deseeded
　　and cut into 1 cm strips
1 avocado, cut into 1 cm slices

## To serve
toasted sesame seeds
chilli flakes (optional)
tamari or coconut aminos*
Sauerkraut (page 177)
wasabi

* See Glossary

Place the mayonnaise and broccoli rice in a bowl and mix to combine. Season with salt and pepper.

Place a nori sheet, rough-side up, on a bench or bamboo sushi mat. Spread one-quarter of the broccoli rice mixture over half the nori, working from the edge closest to you and spreading it out to the sides. Arrange one-quarter of the salmon, cucumber and avocado strips in the middle and dollop on 1 teaspoon of the extra mayonnaise. Starting with the edge closest to you, tightly wrap up the roll. If the nori roll doesn't seal, brush a little water on the inside edge of the nori sheet, then continue to roll to seal. Repeat with the remaining nori, broccoli rice and fillings.

Trim the ends of each nori roll with a sharp knife and cut into 2.5 cm rounds. Sprinkle on the toasted sesame seeds and chilli flakes (if using) and serve with the tamari or coconut aminos, the sauerkraut and the wasabi on the side.

Pâté is without a doubt the most nutritious meal on the planet, and every human culture knows the inherent benefits of its star ingredient: nutrient-dense liver. I wanted to share my love of this superfood with this delicious and easy recipe that kids and adults can enjoy. We like to make up a big batch of pâté, then freeze it in small jars that are the perfect size for lunch. Pack the frozen pâté in the kids' lunch boxes; it will thaw by lunchtime, ready for them to enjoy with crackers, olives and vegetable sticks.

# CHICKEN LIVER PÂTÉ

## SERVES 4–6

3 tablespoons coconut oil or
    good-quality animal fat*, melted
1 onion, chopped
3 small garlic cloves, chopped
1 ½ teaspoons thyme leaves
2 bay leaves
4 sage leaves, chopped
125 ml (½ cup) Chicken Bone Broth
    (page 170)
500 g chicken livers, trimmed
1 tablespoon Dijon mustard
125 ml (½ cup) duck fat, melted
sea salt and freshly ground
    black pepper

### To serve
Sunflower Seed Crackers (page 46)
mixed olives
Lebanese cucumber, cut into sticks
    or slices

* See Glossary

Place 2 tablespoons of the oil or fat, the onion, garlic and thyme in a saucepan over medium–low heat and cook, stirring occasionally, for 10–15 minutes until the onion is softened and slightly caramelised. Add the bay leaves and sage, pour in the bone broth and simmer until reduced to about 2 tablespoons of liquid. Set aside to cool. Remove the bay leaves.

Heat the remaining oil or fat in a large frying pan over medium–high heat, add the livers in batches and cook for 30 seconds on each side until they are brown but still pink in the middle. Remove from the pan and set aside to cool.

Place the cooked livers, the onion and broth reduction and the mustard and duck fat in a blender and blend until smooth. Add salt to taste and blend a few more times to mix through.

Pass the pâté through a fine sieve and add pepper to taste.

Spoon the pâté into glass jars or bowls, leaving 1.5 cm space at the top. Cover and place in the fridge for 4–6 hours to set. Serve the pâté with the crackers, olives and cucumber.

School and work lunches do not have to be difficult, but they should be delicious. Here, we have taken the classic tuna and egg salad and served it in some cos lettuce. To avoid soggy lettuce, pack the salad and cos leaves in separate lunch boxes — you might like to pack a spoon or fork, too — and then assemble your salad cups at lunchtime.

# FISH AND EGG SALAD LETTUCE CUPS

## SERVES 5

185 g tuna, salmon, mackerel or
    sardines in brine or olive oil*,
    drained
6 hard-boiled eggs, chopped
3 tablespoons roughly chopped
    flat-leaf parsley leaves, plus extra
    to serve
60 g (¼ cup) Mayonnaise (page 174),
    plus extra to serve
sea salt and freshly ground
    black pepper
10 baby cos lettuce leaves
1 lemon, cut into wedges

* See Glossary

Place the fish, chopped egg, parsley and mayonnaise in a bowl and gently mix to combine. Season with salt and pepper.

Spoon the salad into the lettuce leaf cups. Top with the extra parsley, squeeze on some lemon juice and add a dollop of extra mayonnaise.

We all know that everything tastes better when it is wrapped, or perhaps it is just the ease of eating with your hands that makes a wrap more appealing. Well, whatever the reason, here we have used a simple nut-free paleo wrap to do the job and added a favourite sandwich filling.

# HAM AND SALAD WRAPS

## MAKES 4

1 large beetroot
4 Paleo Wraps (page 42)
¼ iceberg lettuce (about 150 g),
    leaves separated
125 g (½ cup) Mayonnaise (page 174)
1 avocado, sliced
1 carrot, grated
8 thin slices of leg ham
1 Lebanese cucumber, sliced
1 large tomato, sliced
sea salt and freshly ground
    black pepper

Place the beetroot in a saucepan filled with water and bring to the boil over medium heat. Reduce the heat to medium–low and cook for 40 minutes, or until cooked through. It's ready when a skewer or knife inserted in the middle slips in and slides out easily. Drain, allow cool to slightly and, when cool enough to handle, peel. Allow to cool completely, then cut into 5 mm thick slices, and set aside.

Place the paleo wraps on a work surface. Divide the lettuce among the wraps, dollop on the mayonnaise, then top with the avocado, carrot, ham, cucumber, tomato and beetroot. Season with salt and pepper, roll up each wrap and serve.

I have included a few bread recipes in this book for you to try, as I know a lot of parents want to make sure that the food they pack in their kids' lunch boxes looks just like what the other kids are eating. Here is the king of all sandwiches — the BLT!

# BLT WITH TURKEY

## SERVES 2

1 teaspoon coconut oil or
  good-quality animal fat*
4 rindless bacon rashers
4 sandwich-cut slices of Nut-free
  Paleo Bread (page 49)
60 g (¼ cup) Aioli (page 168) or
  Mayonnaise (page 174)
4 thin slices of turkey (about 60 g)
1 tomato, sliced
2–4 baby cos lettuce leaves, torn
1 small handful of alfalfa sprouts

## Smashed avo

1 avocado
2 teaspoons lemon juice
sea salt and freshly ground
  black pepper

* See Glossary

Heat the oil or fat in a frying pan over medium–high heat. Add the bacon and cook, turning occasionally, until golden and cooked to your liking – cook for about 5 minutes for medium–crisp.

To make the smashed avo, mash the avocado with a fork or a masher until creamy but still slightly chunky. Add the lemon juice and mix until combined, then season with salt and pepper.

To assemble, spread half the smashed avo on two slices of bread, then spread on half the aioli or mayonnaise. Top with the bacon, turkey, tomato, cos and alfalfa, then add the rest of the aioli or mayonnaise and smashed avo and finish with the remaining slices of bread.

## Variation

Use chicken instead of turkey, if you prefer.

Of all the fillings to put into a sandwich, one of my all-time favourites has to be chicken, avocado and lettuce with mayo. You can use leftover roast, poached or grilled chicken — ideally leg meat as it has more flavour, and, of course, include the skin. To take this lunch to the next level, add some sauerkraut and crispy bacon or pork crackling.

# CHICKEN AND AVOCADO ROLLS

## SERVES 4

420 g leftover roast chicken,
   shredded
150 g Mayonnaise (page 174)
½ teaspoon finely grated lemon zest
2 teaspoons lemon juice
1 tablespoon chopped curly or
   flat-leaf parsley leaves
2 teaspoons chopped tarragon leaves
sea salt and freshly ground
   black pepper
4–8 butter lettuce leaves, torn
1 avocado, sliced
4 Nut-free Paleo Bread Round Rolls
   (page 49), sliced in half

Place the chicken, mayo, lemon zest and juice, parsley and tarragon in a bowl and mix well. Season with salt and pepper.

To assemble, divide the butter lettuce leaves, chicken filling and avocado among the rolls and serve.

These days we are so lucky to have butchers, delis, farmers' markets and supermarkets once again stocking and making proper sausages, one of my favourite foods to eat on a weekly basis. And snags encased in a simple thin egg wrap is a fun way to serve them for both kids and adults. Add some raw or cooked veg on the side, and you have a smashing brunch, lunch or picnic idea.

# SAUSAGE ROLL EGG WRAPS

## MAKES 10

1 tablespoon coconut oil or
   good-quality animal fat*
10 gluten- and grain-free beef,
   pork or chicken chipolatas
Tomato Ketchup (page 180),
   to serve

### Egg wraps
6 eggs
3 tablespoons coconut milk
sea salt and freshly ground
   black pepper
3 ½ tablespoons coconut oil or
   good-quality animal fat

* See Glossary

To make the egg wraps, crack the eggs into a bowl, add the coconut milk and whisk with a fork until smooth. Season with a pinch of salt and pepper. Heat 1 teaspoon of the oil or fat in a 20 cm non-stick frying pan over medium heat. Pour in about 60 ml (¼ cup) of egg mixture and tilt and swirl the pan so the mixture covers the base. Cook for 1 minute, or until the egg is just set on top. Slide onto a plate and repeat this process until all the egg mixture is used and you have 5 egg sheets.

Heat the oil or fat in a large frying pan over medium heat. Add the sausages and cook for about 6 minutes until browned on all sides and almost cooked through. Remove the sausages from the pan and set aside.

Cut the egg sheets into 8 cm x 18 cm pieces and transfer to a chopping board with the short side facing you. Place a chipolata crossways at the lower edge of the egg wrap. Tightly wrap, then roll the egg around the chipolata to enclose. (Trim the ends with a sharp knife, if desired). Repeat with the remaining egg wraps and chipolatas. Serve with the tomato ketchup.

We all agree that kids and adults need to increase their vegetable intake, and soups are a great way of achieving this. Instead of focussing on one type of vegetable, as in a pumpkin, mushroom or asparagus soup, let's go the whole hog by including a variety of different veg and serving up this delicious minestrone. You will need to get yourself a good thermos or two for soups in winter — my daughters love taking them to school. You can pack some paleo bread too if the kids like to dip bread in their soup.

# MINESTRONE

## SERVES 6

2 tablespoons coconut oil or
   good-quality animal fat*
2 onions, chopped
2 tablespoons tomato paste
1 large smoked ham hock (800 g–1 kg)
3 garlic cloves, sliced
2 celery stalks, sliced
2 carrots, halved lengthways and
   chopped into 5 mm half moons
1 turnip, cut into 1 cm cubes
1 teaspoon finely chopped
   rosemary leaves
2 litres Chicken Bone Broth
   (page 170)
400 g whole peeled tomatoes
   (see Note), crushed
2 zucchini, cut into 1 cm cubes
300 g butternut pumpkin,
   chopped into 2 cm chunks
1–2 tablespoons lemon juice
sea salt and freshly ground
   black pepper
1 small handful of flat-leaf parsley
   leaves, chopped

* See Glossary

Heat the oil or fat in a large saucepan over medium heat. Add the onion and cook, stirring often, for 3–5 minutes until softened. Add the tomato paste and cook, stirring, for 1 minute. Add the ham hock, garlic, celery, carrot, turnip and rosemary. Pour in the broth and crushed tomatoes and bring to the boil. (The ham hock must be completely submerged during cooking, so add a little more broth or water if necessary.) Reduce the heat to low, cover and simmer for 2½ hours until the meat is just starting to fall off the bone.

Add the zucchini and pumpkin to the pan and cook for a further 30 minutes, or until the zucchini and pumpkin are soft and the meat is falling off the bone.

Remove the ham hock from the soup and, when cool enough to handle, remove the meat from the bone, discarding the skin and fat. Shred or chop the meat and return to the soup. Stir in the lemon juice, season with salt and pepper and sprinkle on the parsley. Ladle the soup into warmed bowls and serve or pour into thermoses.

### Note
I prefer to buy diced and whole peeled tomatoes in jars rather than cans, due to the presence of Bisphenol A (BPA) in many cans. BPA is a toxic chemical that can interfere with our hormonal system.

This interesting and nutritious recipe is perfect for when you feel like a lightish lunch. It is super delicious and quite satisfying, but won't make you feel bloated or lethargic. You can add vegetables if you like or keep it relatively simple as we have here.

# CHICKEN AND PARSLEY BROTH

## SERVES 4

1.25 litres Chicken, Beef or Fish
   Bone Broth (page 170, 168 or 172)
½ onion, sliced
4 chicken thigh fillets or 2 chicken
   breast fillets (about 400 g in total)
1 large handful of flat-leaf parsley
   leaves, finely chopped
½ teaspoon finely grated ginger
   (optional)
½ teaspoon ground cumin (optional)
1 tablespoon lemon juice (optional)
sea salt and freshly ground
   black pepper

Place the broth in a saucepan and bring to a simmer over medium heat. Add the onion and chicken and simmer for 12 minutes, or until the chicken is cooked through.

Remove the chicken from the broth and, when cool enough to handle, shred into bite-sized pieces. Return the shredded chicken to the broth, then stir in the parsley and the ginger, cumin and lemon juice (if using). Season with salt and pepper. Ladle the broth into serving bowls and serve or pour into thermoses for later use.

My mum, Joy, makes a pretty mean chicken and vegetable soup, and the girls ask for it whenever Mum has them to stay. I don't think there is a greater compliment to your cooking than getting requests for a particular dish. I asked Mum for her recipe and she happily agreed to share it with us all. Thanks for your support and help with the girls over the last ten or so years, Mum – looking forward to many more great times together.

# JOY'S CHICKEN AND VEGETABLE SOUP

## SERVES 6–8

5 chicken thighs, bone in or out
2 carrots, chopped
2 celery stalks, chopped
½ sweet potato, chopped
1 zucchini, chopped
1 onion, chopped
450 g pumpkin, chopped
½ teaspoon sweet paprika
½ teaspoon ground turmeric
2 litres Chicken Bone Broth (page 170), vegetable stock or water
1 handful of flat-leaf parsley leaves, chopped
2 handfuls of chopped baby spinach leaves
sea salt and freshly ground black pepper

Place the chicken, carrot, celery, sweet potato, zucchini, onion, pumpkin and spices and the broth, stock or water in a stockpot or slow cooker, bring to a simmer and cook on low for 3 hours.

Carefully remove the chicken from the soup, discard the bones and shred the meat, then set aside.

Using a hand-held blender, blend the soup until slightly smooth (some chunks of veg are fine), then pop the chicken back in. Mix through the parsley and spinach and season with salt and pepper.

Caesar salad is one of those classic dishes adored by everyone. Adding some chicken (or turkey, pork, prawns or lamb) takes it from a side dish and makes it good enough to stand on its own for lunch – or dinner or even breakfast. I recommend storing the dressing separately in your lunch box and adding it when serving, so your salad doesn't go soggy. Leave off the grated macadamia to make this recipe nut free for school.

# CHICKEN CAESAR SALAD

## SERVES 4

4 boneless chicken thighs, skin on
2 tablespoons coconut oil or
    good-quality animal fat*
6 rindless streaky bacon rashers
2 baby cos lettuces, leaves
    separated and torn
1 handful of flat-leaf parsley leaves,
    roughly chopped
4 soft-boiled eggs, peeled and
    cut in half
100 g Sauerkraut (page 177)
2 macadamia nuts, finely grated
    (optional)

## Dressing

100 g Aioli (page 168) or
    Mayonnaise (page 174)
4 anchovy fillets, finely chopped
1 teaspoon lemon juice, plus
    extra if needed
sea salt and freshly ground
    black pepper

* See Glossary

To make the dressing, combine all the ingredients with 1 teaspoon of water in a small bowl. Taste and add a little more lemon juice if needed. Set aside.

Flatten the chicken thighs with a mallet to ensure they cook evenly. Season the skin and flesh generously with salt and pepper.

Melt the oil or fat in a large, heavy-based frying pan over medium–high heat. Place the chicken, skin-side down, in the pan and fry, undisturbed, for 6–8 minutes until crispy and golden brown. Flip the chicken over and cook for 3 minutes, or until cooked through. Remove from the pan and keep warm.

Add the bacon to the pan and cook over medium–high heat for 1–2 minutes on each side until crisp and golden. Remove from the pan and drain on paper towel. Break into bite-sized pieces.

Arrange the lettuce and parsley in a large serving bowl. Slice the chicken, then arrange on the lettuce. Top with the bacon and eggs, add the sauerkraut, then drizzle over the dressing. Sprinkle with salt and pepper and finish with the grated macadamia (if using).

The French know how to cook delicious food and make ingredients shine — and for a great lunch or picnic you don't have to look much further than the classic Niçoise salad. I have taken the liberty of replacing the potato with sweet potato (you could also use parsnip, Jerusalem artichoke, carrot or pumpkin) and, for a greater prebiotic hit, swapped out the beans for some delicious asparagus, which our guts love. Feel free to swap the fish for smoked eel, mussels, prawns or roast pork or chicken.

# SIMPLE NIÇOISE SALAD

## SERVES 4–6

1 sweet potato (about 300 g), peeled and cut into 2.5 cm cubes
2 tablespoons coconut oil or good-quality animal fat*, melted
sea salt and freshly ground black pepper
4 eggs
10 asparagus spears, trimmed and cut into 4 cm lengths
400 g tuna, salmon, mackerel or sardines in brine or olive oil*, drained
250 g mini roma tomatoes, halved
150 g pitted kalamata olives
½ red onion, thinly sliced
1 small handful of flat-leaf parsley leaves
2 large handfuls of mixed salad leaves

### Vinaigrette
1 garlic clove, crushed
1 teaspoon Dijon mustard
3 tablespoons apple cider vinegar
100 ml extra-virgin olive oil

* See Glossary

To make the vinaigrette, combine all the ingredients in a bowl and whisk well. Set aside.

Preheat the oven to 180°C (160°C fan-forced) and line a baking tray with baking paper.

Scatter the sweet potato over the prepared tray in a single layer, drizzle on the oil or fat and season with salt and pepper. Roast, stirring and tossing the sweet potato once or twice, for 20–30 minutes until lightly golden and cooked through. Set aside to cool.

Place the eggs in a large saucepan of water. Bring to the boil over medium heat and simmer for 5½ minutes, or until cooked to your liking.

While the eggs are cooking, place the asparagus in a steamer basket or colander and place on top of the pan. Cover and steam the asparagus for 2 minutes, or until tender but still crisp. Remove from the heat, plunge the asparagus into iced water, then drain well.

Peel the eggs in cold running water, then cut in half and set aside.

To assemble the salad, combine the fish, sweet potato, asparagus, tomatoes, olives, onion, parsley and salad leaves in a large bowl. Season with salt and pepper. Add just enough vinaigrette to moisten the ingredients, then toss gently to coat.

Arrange the salad on a serving platter or individual plates. Place the halved eggs on top, drizzle with the remaining vinaigrette and serve.

Here's my take on the school canteen's pesto pasta: delicious nut-free paleo pesto served with nutritious zucchini noodles and some healthy animal protein and fat. This easy lunch also works well with parsnip noodles and cooked prawns, wild salmon, roast lamb or leftover sausages. Leave off the grated macadamia to make this recipe nut free.

# ZUCCHINI NOODLES WITH CHICKEN AND PESTO

## SERVES 4

80 ml (⅓ cup) coconut oil
600 g chicken thigh fillets
   (about 4), sliced
4–5 zucchini, spiralised into
   thin noodles

## Pesto

2 garlic cloves, chopped
1 large handful of basil leaves,
   plus extra to serve
1 large handful of mint leaves
1 large handful of baby spinach leaves
60 g sunflower seeds, toasted
130 ml olive oil
2 tablespoons lemon juice
sea salt and freshly ground
   black pepper

## To serve

extra-virgin olive oil
lemon wedges
1 macadamia nut, finely grated
   (optional)

To make the pesto, place all the ingredients in the bowl of a food processor and whiz until the herbs and sunflower seeds are finely chopped. Taste and season with a little more salt and pepper if needed.

Melt 2 tablespoons of the coconut oil in a large frying pan over medium–high heat. Season the chicken with salt and pepper and sauté, in batches, for 5 minutes, or until cooked through and slightly golden. Remove the chicken from the pan, set aside and cover with a couple sheets of baking paper or a lid to keep warm.

Wipe the pan clean and place over medium heat. Add the remaining coconut oil and the zucchini noodles and sauté for 1½ minutes, or until the zucchini is almost cooked through. Season with a little salt and pepper. Remove from the heat, add the chicken and pesto and toss to combine.

Transfer the noodle mixture to a large platter or serving plates, drizzle on some extra-virgin olive oil, add a squeeze of lemon juice and sprinkle some grated macadamia over the top, if desired.

Fish cakes for school or work lunches are probably one of the healthiest options around. My girls love these wild salmon cakes. As a parent, I love being able to make a big batch for their lunch boxes. (They make for a wonderful breakfast, too, with a fried egg and some sautéed greens on the side.)

For this recipe, we use a jar of wild salmon, however, you can use pretty much any cooked seafood you wish, or try replacing the salmon with minced chicken, lamb or beef to make a yummy burger patty. Serve with a garden salad, some aioli or mayo and fermented veg and you are in heaven. Oh, and make a lot like I do, so you have leftovers to hand.

# WILD SALMON CAKES

## SERVES 4–5

300 g wild pink or red salmon*,
    in olive oil or brine, drained
190 g (1 cup) Sweet Potato Puree
    (page 179)
2 eggs
finely grated zest of 1 lemon
2 tablespoons coconut flour
1 tablespoon snipped chives
1 tablespoon chopped dill
sea salt and freshly ground
    black pepper
coconut oil, for cooking

### To serve
½ iceberg lettuce, cut into wedges
1 avocado, cut lengthways
    into wedges
cherry tomatoes, halved
Aioli (page 168) or Mayonnaise
    (page 174)
lemon wedges

Combine the salmon, sweet potato puree, eggs, lemon zest, coconut flour and herbs in a bowl. Season to taste with salt and pepper.

Divide the salmon mixture into ten balls, then flatten gently into patties.

Heat a little oil in a frying pan over medium heat. Add half the salmon cakes and fry for 1 minute, or until golden. Turn and fry on the other side for a further 1 minute, or until golden and heated through. Drain on paper towel. Repeat this process for the remaining salmon cakes.

Sprinkle the salmon cakes with a little more salt, if desired. Serve with the lettuce, avocado, tomatoes, aioli or mayonnaise and lemon wedges.

Cabbage leaves make for the best wraps, but it is important to get the right type of cabbage. I like to use savoy or Chinese cabbage as the leaves are tender, thin and subtle in flavour. These meatballs are made with chicken mince and flavoured with Thai spices to give them a nice little lift in flavour. The mint and coriander are paramount for a dish like this, so make sure you pack enough salad in the lunch boxes.

# CHICKEN LARB MEATBALLS IN CABBAGE CUPS

## SERVES 4

coconut oil or good-quality
  animal fat*, for greasing
500 g chicken mince
1 egg
2 red Asian shallots, finely diced
1 long red chilli, deseeded and
  finely chopped
1 spring onion, finely chopped
1 tablespoon finely chopped
  coriander leaves
1½ tablespoons fish sauce
2 tablespoons coconut milk

### Lime and fish sauce dressing
80 ml (⅓ cup) lime juice
3 tablespoons fish sauce
1 long green or red chilli, deseeded
  and finely chopped

### Salad
1 handful of mint leaves, torn
1 handful of coriander leaves, torn
1 handful of Thai basil leaves, torn
1 Lebanese cucumber, deseeded
  and cut into thin matchsticks
2 spring onions, thinly sliced
1 handful of mung bean sprouts

### To serve
8 savoy cabbage leaves
1 tablespoon sesame seeds, toasted
1 lime, cut into cheeks or wedges

* See Glossary

Preheat the oven to 200°C (180°C fan-forced). Grease a 24-hole mini muffin tin with oil or fat.

Place the mince, egg, shallot, chilli, spring onion, coriander, fish sauce and coconut milk in the bowl of a food processor and pulse a few times until the mixture comes together.

Divide the mixture evenly among the holes of the prepared muffin tin. Bake for 13–15 minutes, or until the meatballs are cooked all the way through.

Meanwhile, to make the dressing, combine all the ingredients in a bowl and mix well.

To make the salad, place all the ingredients in a bowl, pour over enough dressing to coat the leaves and gently toss.

To serve, place the cabbage leaf cups on a serving platter or plates. Place a small handful of salad in each cup, then top with 2–3 meatballs. Drizzle over some more dressing, sprinkle on the sesame seeds and serve with the lime.

### Tip
For adults, you may wish to increase the chilli in the meatball mixture or the dressing.

I don't think I've ever met a kid who doesn't love a sausage roll, so it's only fitting that we include two recipes for them in this book. Obviously, the key to this dish is getting the best-quality beef mince you can get your hands on – the fattier the better. There are two gluten-free pastries to choose from here, so you can use nuts or go nut free, depending on your preferences and your school's food policy. Serve with some fresh veggies on the side to complete the meal.

# BEEF AND THYME SAUSAGE ROLLS

## MAKES 12 LARGE OR 24 SMALL

80 ml (⅓ cup) good-quality animal
   fat*, melted
2 onions, chopped
4 garlic cloves, finely chopped
2 teaspoons finely chopped thyme
400 g beef mince
250 g pork mince
100 g (⅔ cup) grated carrot
2 eggs
2 teaspoons Dijon mustard
2 tablespoons Tomato Ketchup
   (page 180), plus extra to serve
2 teaspoons sea salt
2 tablespoons finely chopped flat-leaf
   parsley leaves
1 teaspoon freshly ground black pepper
4 sheets Paleo Pastry (page 175)
   or Nut-free Paleo Pastry
   (page 174)

## Egg wash
1 egg
pinch of sea salt

* See Glossary

To make the egg wash, place the egg, salt and 1 tablespoon of water in a small bowl and whisk until well combined. Set aside.

Preheat the oven to 220°C (200°C fan-forced). Line two baking trays with baking paper.

Heat 2 tablespoons of the fat in a frying pan over medium heat. Add the onion and cook, stirring occasionally, for 5 minutes, or until translucent. Add the garlic and thyme and cook for 1 minute. Remove from the heat and allow to cool completely. Combine the remaining fat with the mince, carrot, egg, mustard, ketchup and salt in the bowl of a food processor and pulse a few times to combine. Add the parsley, pepper, the onion mixture and all the fat from the pan and pulse a couple more times to form a paste. Divide the mixture into four even portions.

Place a pastry sheet on a work surface with the long sides facing you. Gently peel away the top layer of baking paper and, working quickly, pipe one portion of the sausage mixture at a thickness of 4 cm along one long side, leaving a 1 cm gap from the edge. Brush a light coating of egg wash on the pastry and, starting with the edge closest to you and with the bottom sheet of paper still intact, roll up carefully to enclose the filling. When the filling is enclosed, carefully peel way the paper and turn the roll so the seam is underneath, then transfer to a prepared tray. Repeat with the remaining sausage mixture and pastry. Brush the tops of the sausage rolls with the remaining egg wash. Bake for 10 minutes, then rotate the trays and bake for a further 10 minutes until the pastry is golden. Allow to stand for 5 minutes before cutting into 12 large or 24 small sausage rolls. Serve with the extra tomato ketchup.

## Note
You don't need to cook the sausage rolls all at once; you can freeze them uncooked for up to 3 months.

Mmmm, lamb sausage rolls are so good and these have a hint of chilli — remove, reduce or increase, depending on how spicy you and your kids like it. For a really yummy change, you might like to swap the chilli for curry powder or add fresh or dried rosemary, mint or thyme. There are two gluten-free pastries to choose from, so you can use nuts or go nut free.

# CHILLI–LAMB SAUSAGE ROLLS

## MAKES 12

80 ml (⅓ cup) lard or good-quality
   animal fat*
1 onion, finely chopped
1 carrot, grated
1 celery stalk, finely chopped
4 garlic cloves, finely chopped
1 tablespoon finely chopped
   rosemary leaves
1 teaspoon ground cumin
1 teaspoon sweet paprika
1 teaspoon chilli flakes
700 g lamb mince
2 eggs
2 tablespoons Smoked Barbecue
   Sauce (page 178)
2 teaspoons sea salt
1 teaspoon freshly ground black pepper
4 sheets Paleo Pastry (page 175)
   or Nut-free Paleo Pastry
   (page 174)
2 tablespoons sesame seeds
Tomato Ketchup (page 180), to serve

## Egg wash
1 egg
pinch of sea salt

* See Glossary

To make the egg wash, place the egg, salt and 1 tablespoon of water in a small bowl and whisk until well combined. Set aside until needed.

Preheat the oven to 220°C (200°C fan-forced). Line two baking trays with baking paper.

Heat the oil or fat in a frying pan over medium heat. Add the onion, carrot and celery and cook for 8 minutes, or until translucent. Add the garlic and rosemary and cook for 1 minute, then add the cumin, paprika and chilli flakes. Cook, stirring, for 20 seconds, or until fragrant. Allow to cool completely.

Combine the cooled onion mixture, mince, eggs, barbecue sauce, salt and pepper in the bowl of a food processor and process to a paste.

Place a pastry sheet on a work surface with the long sides facing you. Gently peel away the top layer of baking paper and, working quickly, pipe the sausage mixture at a thickness of 4 cm along one long side, leaving a 1 cm gap from the edge. Brush a light coating of egg wash on the pastry and, starting with the edge closest to you and with the bottom sheet of paper still intact, roll up carefully to enclose the filling. When the filling is enclosed, carefully peel away the paper and turn the roll so the seam is underneath, then transfer to a prepared tray. Repeat with the remaining meat mixture and pastry sheets. Brush the tops of the sausage rolls with the remaining egg wash, then sprinkle on the sesame seeds. Bake for 10 minutes, then brush the tops with another light coating of egg wash, rotate the trays and bake for a further 10 minutes until the pastry is golden. Allow to stand for 5 minutes before cutting into 12 portions and serving with the tomato ketchup.

## Note
You can freeze uncooked sausage rolls for up to 3 months.

This indulgent recipe — our interpretation of the classic breakfast muffin found in fast-food establishments around the globe — dispels the preconception that paleo food is boring, tasteless and not fun. Our version removes the most common inflammatory ingredients, such as gluten, grains, dairy and toxic oils, and replaces them with healthy fats and protein. Serve with some fresh veggies, salad or sauerkraut on the side.

# SAUSAGE, BACON AND EGG MUFFINS

## SERVES 4

3 tablespoons coconut oil or
   good-quality animal fat*
4 rindless bacon rashers
4 eggs
sea salt and freshly ground
   black pepper
4 English Muffins (page 56), halved
80 g Mayonnaise (page 174)
80 g Tomato Ketchup (page 180)

### Patties
130 g full-fat beef mince
100 g full-fat pork mince
1 tablespoon lard, melted
½ teaspoon onion powder
½ teaspoon garlic powder
¼ teaspoon dried thyme
1 egg
pinch of chilli flakes (optional)
sea salt and freshly ground
   black pepper

### To serve
pickles
Vegetable Crisps (we used parsnip,
   see page 34)

* See Glossary

To make the patties, combine all the ingredients in a large bowl and mix well. Season to taste, then shape into four even patties.

Heat a barbecue plate or chargrill pan to medium–high. Brush with 2 tablespoons of the oil or fat, add the patties and bacon and cook for 2 minutes. Turn the patties and bacon and continue to cook for a couple of minutes until the patties are cooked through and the bacon is crisp. Remove from the heat and keep warm.

Heat the remaining oil or fat on the barbecue or in a large frying pan, add the eggs and cook for 2 minutes until the whites are set and the yolks are still runny. Season with a little salt and pepper, then flip over and cook for a further 10 seconds to seal. Remove from the heat and keep warm.

Meanwhile, toast the muffins, flat-side down, on the barbecue or in the pan until golden brown.

Spread the mayonnaise over four toasted muffin halves and layer on the bacon, patties, egg and tomato ketchup, then top with the remaining muffin halves. Serve with the pickles and parsnip crisps.

Recently, we have been making a lot of Indian food, as I love using spices and herbs in my cooking. Bhajis have become a go-to quick and delicious lunch for us. Here, we have added zucchini to the classic onion bhaji, but you can include any vegetable you love, and also add some bacon, chicken or fish if you like. These bhajis are just as yummy, or even yummier, cold the next day.

# ZUCCHINI AND ONION BHAJIS

## MAKES 14

400 g coarsely grated zucchini (about 1 large)
1 teaspoon fine sea salt
½ onion, thinly sliced
3 eggs
2 tablespoons tapioca flour*
2 tablespoons coconut flour
½ teaspoon bicarbonate of soda
1½ teaspoons ground cumin
1½ teaspoons ground coriander
¼ teaspoon chilli powder or a pinch of cayenne pepper (optional)
sea salt and freshly ground black pepper
250 ml (1 cup) coconut oil or good-quality animal fat*
Curried Mayonnaise (page 64), to serve
lemon cheeks or wedges, to serve

* See Glossary

Place the zucchini in a colander, sprinkle with the salt and mix to combine. Leave the zucchini to 'sweat' for 15 minutes.

Squeeze out all the moisture from the zucchini with your hands. You can also wrap the zucchini in a clean tea towel or some cheesecloth and squeeze out the liquid.

Combine the zucchini, onion, eggs, tapioca and coconut flours, bicarbonate of soda, cumin, coriander and chilli powder or cayenne pepper (if using) in a bowl and mix well to form a thick batter. Season with salt and pepper.

Heat the oil or fat in a large, deep frying pan over medium heat. Test the heat of the oil or fat by placing a small amount of batter in the pan. If the oil or fat begins to sizzle around the bhaji mixture, it has reached its ideal heat. Gently drop 1 tablespoon of batter per bhaji into the pan (don't cook more than four per batch) and cook for 2 minutes on each side, or until golden brown and cooked through. Remove the bhajis from the pan using metal tongs or a slotted spoon and drain on paper towel. Sprinkle with salt and allow the bhajis to cool for 1 minute before serving with the curried mayonnaise and lemon cheeks or wedges.

Really simple but delicious is how I sum up this recipe. And we all know how much kids of any age love a good chicken nugget. Feel free to make your own sauce/s to accompany these, like a homemade paleo barbecue or tomato sauce or perhaps some curry mayo, pesto or chimichurri. You may wish to serve these with some lettuce leaves to make wraps, or try a salad on the side, or add some guacamole for dipping. The chicken can be replaced with any other animal mince, such as pork, fish, lamb, beef or duck.

# CHICKEN NUGGETS

## MAKES 30

500 g chicken mince
1 small carrot (about 130 g), grated
1 small zucchini (about 130 g), grated
2 garlic cloves, finely chopped
sea salt and freshly ground
    black pepper
80 ml (⅓ cup) coconut oil or
    good-quality animal fat*

### To serve
Mayonnaise (page 174)
cherry tomatoes, halved
veggie sticks of your choice (optional)

* See Glossary

Place the chicken, carrot, zucchini and garlic in the bowl of a food processor and pulse a few times until finely chopped and combined. Season with salt and pepper.

Roll 1 tablespoon of the chicken mixture into a ball, then flatten slightly to form a nugget shape.

Heat the oil or fat in a large non-stick frying pan over medium heat. Add the chicken nuggets in batches and fry for 2½ minutes on each side, or until golden and cooked through. Drain on paper towel. Season with a little more salt, if desired.

Serve the nuggets with the mayonnaise and cherry tomatoes or with some veggie sticks, if you prefer.

This is one of my girls' all-time favourite dinners, so we often send them to school the next day with leftovers. Cold Mexican mince is delicious with sweet potato crisps or seed crackers, some guacamole and vegetables, such as carrot, celery, tomato and cucumber.

# PALEO NACHOS

**SERVES 4**

**Spicy Mexican beef**
2 tablespoons coconut oil or
   good-quality animal fat*
2 onions, finely chopped
2 garlic cloves, finely chopped
1 long red chilli, deseeded and chopped
500 g beef mince
1 teaspoon smoked paprika
1 teaspoon ground cumin
½ teaspoon ground coriander
1½ tablespoons tomato paste
400 g diced tomatoes
   (see Note page 107)
sea salt and freshly ground
   black pepper

**Salad**
1 baby cos lettuce, leaves separated
   and torn
1 Lebanese cucumber, halved
   lengthways and sliced
12 cherry tomatoes, halved
8 yellow teardrop tomatoes, halved
1 tablespoon apple cider vinegar
2 tablespoons extra-virgin olive oil

**To serve**
Vegetable Crisps (we used sweet
   potato, see page 34)
1 handful of coriander leaves
Guacamole (page 173)

* See Glossary

To make the spicy Mexican beef, heat the oil or fat in a frying pan over medium–high heat. Add the onion and cook for 5 minutes, or until translucent. Stir in the garlic and chilli and cook for 1 minute, or until fragrant. Add the beef and cook, stirring with a wooden spoon to break up any lumps, for 5 minutes until browned. Add the spices and tomato paste and cook for 1 minute, then mix in the tomatoes and 125 ml (½ cup) of water. Reduce the heat to low and simmer for 10–12 minutes. Season with salt and pepper.

To make the salad, place the cos, cucumber and tomatoes in a bowl. Add the vinegar and olive oil and gently toss to coat. Season with salt and pepper.

Place the sweet potato crisps on serving plates or in lunch boxes, top with the spicy beef and a sprinkle of coriander leaves and serve with the salad and guacamole on the side.

**Tip**
For added goodness, use beef or chicken broth instead of water in the spicy Mexican beef.

When avocados are wonderfully ripe, in season and affordable, there really is no better time to pack them in lunch boxes with assorted fillings. This Mexican beef combo and the BLT recipe overleaf are two of my favourites to inspire you. Please feel free to create your own versions that make you and your family smile.

# MEXICAN BEEF MINCE WITH AVO TACOS

## SERVES 2–4

4 iceberg lettuce leaves, cut into cups
2 avocados, halved, stones and
   skin removed
1 x quantity Spicy Mexican Beef
   (see page 132)
½ Lebanese cucumber,
   sliced lengthways and
   cut into matchsticks
a few coriander sprigs
lime cheeks, to serve

### Tomato salsa

2 tomatoes, deseeded and diced
½ red onion, finely diced
2 tablespoons chopped coriander
   leaves, plus extra to serve
2 tablespoons lime juice
2 tablespoons extra-virgin olive oil
sea salt and freshly ground
   black pepper

To make the tomato salsa, place all the ingredients in a bowl and mix well.

To serve, place the lettuce cups on plates or in lunch containers. Top each with an avocado half, then spoon on the spicy Mexican beef, top with the cucumber and coriander and serve with the tomato salsa and lime cheeks on the side.

This could very well become one of your favourite dishes for breakfast, lunch or dinner, or as a handy snack for yourself or the kids when you get home from school or work. You seriously have to try it for yourself to understand how freakin' yummy it is ... and how easy! You can swap the chook for cooked prawns or any other meat that you love.

# AVOCADO BOWL WITH BLT, CHICKEN AND EGG

## SERVES 4

5 rindless streaky bacon rashers
400 g leftover roast chicken, chopped
2 roma tomatoes, chopped
4 hard-boiled eggs, chopped
1 tablespoon chopped curly parsley leaves
100 g Mayonnaise (page 174)
1 baby gem lettuce, leaves separated and torn
sea salt and freshly ground black pepper
2 avocados, halved and stones removed
extra-virgin olive oil, to drizzle

Preheat the oven to 200°C (180°C fan-forced). Grease and line a baking tray with baking paper.

Place the bacon in a single layer on the prepared tray, making sure the strips are not touching. Bake, turning the tray once, for 12–15 minutes until the bacon is golden and crisp. Allow to cool completely, then cut into small pieces.

Combine the bacon, chicken, tomato, egg, parsley and mayonnaise in a bowl and mix well, then add the lettuce and toss gently to coat. Season with salt and pepper.

Without cutting through to the skin, make cross hatch cuts about 1 cm apart in the avocado halves. Spoon the salad into the cavity of each avocado half, drizzle with some oil and sprinkle with more pepper if you like.

There is nothing new about this recipe; it is a family favourite all around Australia. I encourage everyone to make this for a weeknight meal and cook extra to pack for lunch the next day. If you like, as an alternative, you can take the meat off the bone and stir it through cauliflower fried rice.

# HONEY, GINGER AND SOY CHICKEN DRUMSTICKS

## SERVES 4

4 garlic cloves, finely chopped
1 tablespoon finely grated ginger
½ teaspoon Chinese five spice
100 g honey
100 ml tamari or coconut aminos*
2 tablespoons coconut oil or
    good-quality animal fat*, melted
8 chicken drumsticks
1 Lebanese cucumber, cut into sticks
1 teaspoon finely snipped chives
1 tablespoon sesame seeds, toasted
1 x quantity Cauliflower Rice
    (page 169)
1 avocado, diced
1 toasted nori sheet*, cut into strips
1 spring onion, thinly sliced
100 g Mayonnaise (page 174)

* See Glossary

Combine the garlic, ginger, Chinese five spice, honey, tamari or coconut aminos and the oil or fat in a bowl. Mix well, then add the chicken and mix through to coat. Marinate for at least 2 hours in the fridge or, for best results, overnight.

Preheat the oven to 200°C (180°C fan-forced).

Place the chicken in a casserole dish and pour over the marinade. Bake for 20 minutes, then flip the chicken over and continue to cook for 25 minutes, or until the chicken is dark golden brown and cooked through.

Divide the chicken and cucumber among four bowls or lunch boxes, then sprinkle on the chives and half the sesame seeds. Place the cauliflower rice in separate bowls or lunch boxes, top with the avocado and nori, then sprinkle on the spring onion and the remaining sesame seeds. Serve with the mayonnaise on the side.

If you have never made this Japanese cabbage pancake dish before, I encourage you to give it a go. It may just become a new staple for you! I have kept mine super basic with cabbage and bacon, but you can be as adventurous as you like with the fillings – it needs good-quality mayonnaise and teriyaki sauce, which are simple to make yourself. I have included nori, too. Traditionally, okonomiyaki are served with bonito flakes; add these if you want to go all out.

# OKONOMIYAKI

## SERVES 4–5

6 eggs
2 tablespoons coconut flour
1 teaspoon baking powder
1 tablespoon tamari or
    coconut aminos*
½ teaspoon toasted sesame oil
150 g green cabbage, finely shredded
    on a mandoline
2 spring onions, thinly sliced (keep
    white and green parts separate)
80 g rindless bacon, diced
sea salt and freshly ground
    black pepper
3 tablespoons coconut oil or
    good-quality animal fat*

### To serve
2 ½ toasted nori sheets*, cut into
    5 cm squares
125 ml (½ cup) Teriyaki Sauce
    (page 179)
200 g Mayonnaise (page 174) or
    Curried Mayonnaise (see page 64)

* See Glossary

Whisk the eggs, coconut flour, baking powder, tamari or coconut aminos and the sesame oil in a bowl until there are no lumps. Add the cabbage, spring onion whites and bacon and mix well to combine. Season with a little salt and pepper.

Place a large non-stick frying pan over medium heat and add half the oil or fat. Ladle in 1 heaped tablespoon of batter for each pancake and spread out gently with the back of a spoon until 5–6 cm in diameter (cook four pancakes at a time). Cook for 1½–2 minutes on each side until the tops dry out slightly and the bottoms start to brown. Flip and cook for an additional 1½–2 minutes. Repeat with the remaining oil and pancake batter to make about 15 pancakes.

Top each pancake with a nori square, then drizzle on some teriyaki sauce, sprinkle with the spring onion greens and serve with your choice of mayonnaise.

We are so lucky to have some great-quality organic hot dogs available in butchers and supermarkets now, which helps to make packed lunches easier and tastier. Here, for a lighter lunch, we have teamed the hot dogs with lettuce cups; if you and your family feel like something heartier, use seeded rolls instead – these are delicious either way. Please feel free to mix things up from time to time depending on your preferences.

# PALEO HOT DOGS

## SERVES 4

2 ½ tablespoons coconut oil or
   good-quality animal fat*, plus
   extra if needed
1 large onion, sliced
sea salt and freshly ground
   black pepper
2 rindless bacon rashers, chopped
4 beef hot dogs
4 baby cos lettuce leaves  or
   4 Nut-free Paleo Bread Long Rolls
   (page 49)
120 g Sauerkraut (page 177)
80 g (¼ cup) Tomato Ketchup
   (page 180)
3 tablespoons English mustard or
   Dijon mustard

* See Glossary

Melt 2 tablespoons of the oil or fat in a non-stick frying pan over medium heat. Add the onion and sauté for 8 minutes, or until translucent and starting to caramelise. Season with salt and pepper, then remove from the pan and set aside, keeping warm.

Wipe the pan clean with paper towel. Place the pan over medium heat, add the remaining fat or oil and the bacon and cook, stirring occasionally, for 6–8 minutes until the bacon is golden and slightly crispy. Set aside, keeping warm.

Fill a saucepan with water and bring to a gentle simmer (do not boil). Add the hot dogs and cook for 6 minutes, or until heated through. Carefully remove the hot dogs with a slotted spoon or tongs and place on paper towel to drain. Alternatively, heat about 1 tablespoon of extra oil or fat in a non-stick frying pan over medium heat. Add the hot dogs and cook for 6–8 minutes until heated through and lightly coloured all over. Set aside, keeping warm.

Place a hot dog lengthways in the centre of a lettuce leaf. Alternatively, if using the seeded rolls, cut the rolls almost in half lengthways. Do not cut all the way through. Slightly open up and place a hot dog lengthways in each roll. Alternatively, . Scatter over the onion, bacon and sauerkraut, then squeeze on some ketchup, add some mustard and serve.

COUGH DROP GUMMIES

NUT-FREE BANANA BREAD

BLISS BALLS

NUT-FREE MUESLI BARS

SEEDELLA

CHOCOLATE-CHIP COOKIES

RASPBERRY 'BOUNTY' BARS

MINT CHOCOLATE CUPS

COCONUT SNOWBALLS

CHIA SEED PUDDINGS WITH BANANA
AND PASSIONFRUIT

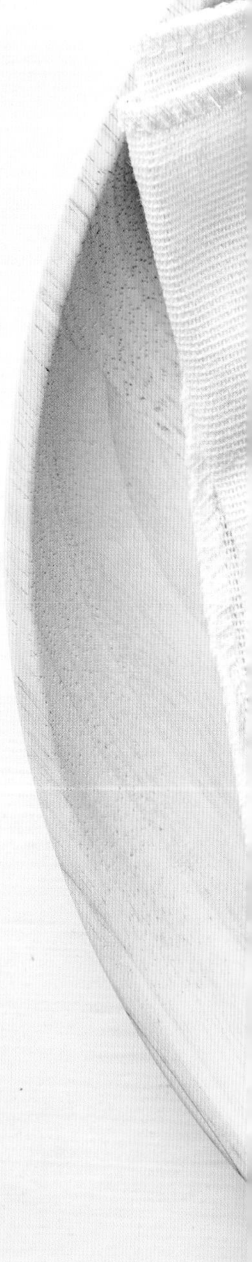

Here, we have created a treat with medicinal properties to soothe sore throats.
These gummies have an amazing taste and texture that the whole family will love.
And, best of all, they have gut-healing gelatine in them.

# COUGH DROP GUMMIES

## MAKES 40

390 ml filtered water
2 lemongrass stems, pale part only,
  bruised with the back of a knife
5 cm piece of ginger, chopped
½ teaspoon ground turmeric
pinch of ground cloves
50 g powdered gelatine
3 tablespoons lemon juice
3 tablespoons honey
  (we use manuka honey)

Place 190 ml of the filtered water and the lemongrass, ginger, turmeric and cloves in a small saucepan. Stir and bring to the boil over medium heat. Turn off the heat, cover with the lid and allow to stand for 1 hour so the flavours infuse.

Meanwhile, sprinkle the gelatine over the remaining 200 ml of water, mix well and allow to stand for at least 5 minutes for the gelatine granules to expand and soften.

Bring the lemongrass and ginger–infused water to a simmer over medium–low heat, stir through the gelatine mixture and continue to stir for 3 minutes, or until the gelatine has completely dissolved. Remove from the heat, then stir through the lemon juice and honey and mix until the honey dissolves.

Pass the liquid through a fine strainer, discard the lemongrass and ginger, then pour into a silicone ice-cube tray or mini silicone moulds. Transfer to the freezer for 15 minutes, or until set. Remove the gummies from the moulds and store in the fridge in an airtight container for up to 2 weeks.

Banana bread has become a popular treat for many kids and adults. With this recipe, we have created a healthier option that is nut free, so it can be taken to school. Having said that, this still contains a high amount of natural sugars and should be viewed as a treat to enjoy in small quantities from time to time.

# NUT-FREE BANANA BREAD

## MAKES 1 X 20 CM LOAF

3 tablespoons coconut oil, melted, plus extra for greasing and serving
80 g coconut flour
1 teaspoon bicarbonate of soda
1 teaspoon ground cinnamon
pinch of sea salt
6 very ripe bananas
4 eggs
¼ teaspoon vanilla powder or 1 vanilla pod, split and seeds scraped
90 g (¼ cup) honey, plus extra for brushing
1 tablespoon apple cider vinegar

Preheat the oven to 180°C (160°C fan-forced). Grease a 20 cm × 10 cm loaf tin with a little coconut oil, then line the base and sides with baking paper.

In a large bowl, combine the coconut flour, bicarbonate of soda, cinnamon and salt and mix well.

Place five bananas in a bowl and mash thoroughly. Slice the remaining banana diagonally into eight pieces. Set aside.

In another bowl, whisk together the eggs, vanilla, honey and vinegar, then stir in the mashed banana.

Pour the liquid ingredients into the dry ingredients and stir with a wooden spoon until thoroughly combined. Add the coconut oil and continue stirring until incorporated.

Spoon the batter into the prepared loaf tin and spread out evenly with a spatula. Arrange the reserved banana slices on top and bake for 1 hour, or until a skewer inserted in the centre comes out clean. Allow the bread to cool in the tin for 10 minutes, then carefully turn out onto a wire rack. Brush a little extra honey over the top and allow to cool for 20–30 minutes. Slice and serve toasted, spread with some coconut oil.

Bliss balls have become popular in a huge way in the last few years – and they are delicious. Here is a nut-free, school-friendly recipe. Feel free to roll them into smaller balls, and, as they are a treat, you may want to pack only one in the lunch box.

# BLISS BALLS

## MAKES 12

40 g (⅔ cup) shredded coconut
60 g (½ cup) ground flaxseeds
60 g (½ cup) sunflower seeds
60 g (½ cup) pumpkin seeds
½ teaspoon vanilla powder or 2 vanilla
    pods, split and seeds scraped
2 teaspoons chia seeds
    (black or white)
2 tablespoons honey or maple syrup
60 g pitted dates (about 4)
60 g (½ cup) dried cranberries

### Crumb

1 tablespoon flaxseeds
3 tablespoons shredded coconut
2 tablespoons pumpkin seeds
2 tablespoons sunflower seeds

To make the crumb, place all the ingredients in the bowl of a food processor and pulse 2–3 times until coarsely chopped. Remove from the food processor and set aside until needed.

Place all the bliss ball ingredients in the bowl of the food processor and blend until the mixture is finely chopped, well combined and sticky. Divide into walnut-sized portions. Lightly wet the palms of your hands and roll into balls. Then roll in the crumb mixture, cover with plastic wrap and place in the fridge for 20 minutes to set. Eat straight away or store in an airtight container in the fridge for up to 2 weeks.

There are many muesli bars on the market that may not be providing your children with the best nutrition. I wanted to create a nut-free paleo muesli bar for schoolkids so they can have something with a wonderful flavour and mouthfeel that's free of nasties. I hope you and your family enjoy this recipe as an occasional treat.

# NUT-FREE MUESLI BARS

## MAKES ABOUT 10

1 ripe banana, roughly chopped
100 ml coconut oil, melted
90 g cacao butter, melted
80 g hulled tahini
100 g honey or 100 ml maple syrup
¼ teaspoon sea salt
1½ teaspoons ground cinnamon
125 g pumpkin seeds
125 g (1 cup) sunflower seeds
2 tablespoons chia seeds
2 tablespoons flaxseeds
3 tablespoons sesame seeds, toasted
60 g (1 cup) shredded coconut
3 tablespoons currants

Line the base and sides of a 24 cm x 18 cm baking tin with baking paper.

Place the banana, coconut oil, cacao butter, tahini, honey or maple syrup, salt and cinnamon in the bowl of a food processor and blend to a smooth, runny paste.

Place the seeds in a large bowl, then stir in the shredded coconut. Pour over the banana mixture and mix until well combined.

Spoon the seed mixture into the prepared tin and smooth using a palette knife or spatula, then evenly sprinkle the currants over the top. Cover and refrigerate for 2–3 hours until set. Cut into even-sized bars and store in an airtight container in the fridge for up to 1 week.

My daughters tell me that many kids come to school with Nutella and white bread sandwiches packed in their lunch boxes. It is really surprising in this day and age that white or even grain bread is still being used, let alone with sugar-laden Nutella! Enjoy this nut-free 'Nutella' – or seedella – instead, spread over nutritious seeded bread or crackers and topped with some sliced banana, if you like.

# SEEDELLA

## MAKES 450 G

220 g (1¾ cups) sunflower seeds
2 tablespoons olive oil
30 g (¼ cup) cacao or carob powder
125 ml (½ cup) maple syrup
pinch of fine sea salt
120 ml coconut milk

Place the sunflower seeds in the bowl of a high-speed blender or food processor and process for about 1 minute to a fine, powdery consistency. Add the olive oil and whiz for 1 minute, occasionally scraping down the side of the bowl, until the mixture forms a thick paste. Next, add the remaining ingredients and blend, occasionally scraping down the side of the bowl, for about 3 minutes until a smooth, spreadable paste forms.

Store in sealed glass jars in the fridge for up to 2 weeks.

Who doesn't love a cookie? Especially when they are free of gluten and refined sugar.
And to top it off, let's make them nut free so that kids can take them to school as
a treat from time to time.

# CHOCOLATE-CHIP COOKIES

## MAKES 12

70 g (½ cup) coconut flour
85 g tapioca flour*
½ teaspoon fine sea salt
2 teaspoons cacao or carob powder
1 teaspoon bicarbonate of soda
180 ml coconut oil, melted
185 ml (¾ cup) maple syrup
½ teaspoon vanilla powder or
   2 teaspoons natural vanilla extract
2 eggs, beaten
180 g dark (70–100% cacao)
   chocolate, chopped into small
   pieces (see Note)

* See Glossary

Preheat the oven to 180°C (160°C fan-forced).
Line two large baking trays with baking paper.

In a large bowl, combine the coconut and tapioca flours,
salt, cacao or carob and bicarbonate of soda and mix
well. Add the coconut oil, maple syrup, vanilla, eggs and
chopped chocolate and mix to form a thick, wet mixture.
Cover with plastic wrap and place in the fridge for
15 minutes to firm up and form a dough.

Divide the dough evenly into 12 pieces, then roll into golf
ball–sized balls and place on the prepared trays, allowing
room for spreading. Gently press down on each dough
ball with a fork. Bake for 15–18 minutes until golden. Cool
on the tray. Serve or store in an airtight container in the
pantry for up to 5 days.

### Note
Make sure the dark chocolate you use for this recipe is
free of both sugar and dairy.

Recently, a parent following a paleo lifestyle asked me what she could do to make her kids feel less alienated at school when it comes to their lunch. I suggested she pack some extra paleo treats for her kids to hand out to their mates. These paleo 'bounty' bars are perfect for school lunch boxes and sharing with friends.

# RASPBERRY 'BOUNTY' BARS

## MAKES 30

330 g (4 cups) shredded coconut
270 ml coconut milk
80 g honey or 80 ml maple syrup
200 g frozen raspberries, thawed
200 ml coconut oil, melted
250 g dark (70–100% cacao)
    chocolate, chopped (see Note)

Line a tray with baking paper.

Place the shredded coconut in the bowl of a food processor and blitz into crumbs. Add the coconut milk, honey or maple syrup, raspberries and coconut oil and whiz for 30 seconds to combine.

Tear off a couple of 30 cm x 15 cm sheets of baking paper from your roll. Place one sheet of paper on a work bench, long side facing you. Working from the edge closest to you, spoon about 4 tablespoons of the mixture across the sheet horizontally, leaving a 1 cm gap from the edge. Starting with the edge closest to you, begin to tightly wrap and roll all the way to the end of the paper to form a log. Smooth the outside of the log with your fingers to remove any air pockets. Gently lift and place on a flat tray, then repeat with the remaining mixture until it is all used up. Place the logs in the fridge to set for 1 hour.

Meanwhile, melt the chocolate in a heatproof bowl over a saucepan of just-simmering water. (Make sure the bowl doesn't touch the water or it will overheat.)

Remove the raspberry and coconut logs from the fridge and cut into roughly 5 cm bars. Dip a dessertspoon into the melted chocolate and drizzle it over the bars. Return to the fridge for 30 minutes, or until the chocolate is set. Store in an airtight container in the fridge for up to 1 week or freeze for up to 3 months.

### Note
Make sure the dark chocolate you use for this recipe is free of both sugar and dairy.

One of my favourite childhood treats was going with my mum to our local Chinese restaurant on the Gold Coast and having a great feed. At the end of the meal, we were always given a chocolate and mint wafer. The purpose of this book is to ensure that kids following a paleo lifestyle can also have wonderful food memories that are delicious and fun. I am sure you and your family will love this recipe.

# MINT CHOCOLATE CUPS

## MAKES 24

olive oil, for greasing
240 g (3 cups) desiccated coconut
250 ml (1 cup) coconut milk
100 g honey or 100 ml maple syrup
8 drops of food-grade peppermint oil
1 tablespoon liquid chlorophyll*
100 ml coconut oil, melted
250 g dark (70–100% cacao)
    chocolate, chopped (see Note)

* See Glossary

Grease two 12-hole round-base standard muffin tins (or any mould shape you like) with olive oil.

Place the desiccated coconut, coconut milk, honey or maple syrup, peppermint oil, chlorophyll and coconut oil in a large bowl and mix to combine.

Spoon 1 tablespoon of the coconut mixture evenly into the muffin holes, flatten the tops with a spoon, then place in the fridge for 1 hour to set.

Meanwhile, melt the chocolate in a heatproof bowl over a saucepan of just-simmering water. (Make sure the bowl doesn't touch the water or it will overheat.)

Line a tray with baking paper and place a wire rack on top. Lightly brush the rack with olive oil.

Pop the peppermint coconut cups out of the tin. Dip their rounded bases in the melted chocolate to coat, then place on the prepared rack, chocolate-side up. (Some excess chocolate will drip onto the tray; this can be reused.) Return to the fridge to set for 20 minutes. Eat or store in an airtight container in the fridge for up to 3 weeks or freeze for up to 6 months.

### Note
Make sure the dark chocolate you use for this recipe is free of both sugar and dairy.

Try serving these at your next party, school fete or work fundraising bake-off.
They look amazing, taste just as good and are pretty damn easy to put together if you
can get the kids – or any member of the family – to help out in the kitchen.

# COCONUT SNOWBALLS

## MAKES 12

120 g (2 cups) shredded coconut,
　　plus 50 g extra for rolling
3 tablespoons coconut oil, melted
3 tablespoons maple syrup
2 tablespoons coconut milk
¼ teaspoon vanilla powder or
　　½ teaspoon natural vanilla
　　extract
½ teaspoon ground cinnamon
pinch of sea salt

Place the shredded coconut and coconut oil in the bowl of
a food processor. Process on high, scraping down the side
of the bowl now and then, for 2 minutes, or until a thick
and grainy paste forms. Add the maple syrup, coconut milk,
vanilla, cinnamon and salt and process until well combined.
Place in the fridge for 15 minutes to set. Shape the mixture
into walnut-sized balls and roll in the extra shredded
coconut to coat. Cover and refrigerate for 30 minutes.
Eat at once or store in an airtight container in the fridge
for up to 1 week.

### Variation
To make beetroot snowballs, add 100 g grated beetroot to
the shredded coconut and coconut oil and process, then
continue with the method above.

This is one of the easiest recipes in the book, and you can change up the fruit according to what's in season. Please note that chia seeds can sometimes affect people's guts, so always listen to your body. Ask yourself and your children how you feel after eating chia seeds. If you get the thumbs-up, then this makes for a great breakfast, little lunch, after-school snack or dessert from time to time.

# CHIA SEED PUDDINGS WITH BANANA AND PASSIONFRUIT

## SERVES 2–4

250 ml (1 cup) coconut milk
50 g (⅓ cup) chia seeds
3 tablespoons honey, or to taste
1 banana, sliced
pulp of 1 passionfruit

Pour the coconut milk into a bowl, add the chia seeds and honey and mix well.

Transfer the chia mixture to small cups or glasses and refrigerate for 2 hours, or until the chia seeds have swollen and formed a thick pudding. Serve with the sliced banana and a drizzle of passionfruit pulp.

### Tip
You might like to mix the passionfruit pulp with ½ teaspoon of honey before drizzling over your chia seed puddings.

AIOLI

BEEF BONE BROTH

BROCCOLI RICE

CAULIFLOWER RICE

CHICKEN BONE BROTH

COCONUT FLOUR TORTILLAS

COCONUT YOGHURT

CRISPY CURRY LEAVES

FISH BONE BROTH

GUACAMOLE

KALE CHIPS

MAYONNAISE

MINT JELLY

NUT-FREE PALEO PASTRY

PALEO PASTRY

RAITA

RENDERED ANIMAL FAT

SAUERKRAUT

SEMI-DRIED TOMATOES

SMOKED BARBECUE SAUCE

SWEET POTATO PUREE

TERIYAKI SAUCE

TOMATO KETCHUP

WORCESTERSHIRE SAUCE

# AIOLI

**MAKES 470 G**

6 roasted garlic cloves
4 egg yolks
2 teaspoons Dijon mustard
2 teaspoons apple cider vinegar
1½ tablespoons lemon juice
420 ml (1⅔ cups) olive oil
sea salt and freshly ground
    black pepper

Combine the garlic, egg yolks, mustard, vinegar, lemon juice and oil in a glass jug or jar. Using a hand-held blender, blend, working the blade from the bottom of the jug slowly to the top, until thick and creamy. Alternatively, place the garlic, egg yolks, mustard, vinegar and lemon juice in the bowl of a food processor and process until combined. With the motor running, slowly pour in the oil in a thin, steady stream and process until the aioli is thick and creamy.

Season with salt and pepper. Store in an airtight container in the fridge for 4–5 days.

# BEEF BONE BROTH

**MAKES 3.5–4 LITRES**

about 2 kg beef knuckle and
    marrow bones
1 calf foot, chopped into pieces
    (optional)
3 tablespoons apple cider vinegar
1.5 kg meaty beef rib or neck bones
3 onions, roughly chopped
3 carrots, roughly chopped
3 celery stalks, roughly chopped
2 leeks, white part only,
    roughly chopped
3 thyme sprigs
2 bay leaves
1 teaspoon black peppercorns, crushed
1 garlic bulb, cut in half horizontally
2 large handfuls of flat-leaf
    parsley stalks

Place the knuckle and marrow bones and calf foot (if using) in a stockpot, add the vinegar and pour in 5 litres of cold water, or enough to cover. Set aside for 1 hour to help draw out the nutrients from the bones. Remove the bones from the pot, reserving the water in a separate container.

Preheat the oven to 180°C (160°C fan-forced).

Place the knuckle and marrow bones, calf foot (if using) and meaty bones in a few large roasting tins and roast in the oven for 30–40 minutes until well browned. Return all the bones to the stockpot and add the vegetables.

Pour the fat from the roasting tins into a saucepan, add 1 litre of the reserved water, place over high heat and bring to a simmer, stirring with a wooden spoon to loosen any coagulated juices. Add this liquid to the bones and vegetables. If necessary, add the remaining reserved water to the pot to just cover the bones – the liquid should come no higher than 2 cm below the rim of the pot, as the volume will increase slightly during cooking.

Bring the broth to the boil, skimming off the scum that rises to the top. Reduce the heat to low and add the thyme, bay leaves, peppercorns and garlic. Simmer for

*continued* >

12–24 hours. Just before finishing, add the parsley and simmer for 10 minutes. Strain the broth into a large container, cover and place in the fridge overnight. Remove the congealed fat that rises to the top and reserve for cooking; it will keep in the fridge for up to 1 week or in the freezer for up to 3 months. Transfer the thick and gelatinous broth to smaller airtight containers and place in the fridge or, for long-term storage, the freezer. The broth can be stored in the fridge for 3–4 days or freezer for up to 3 months.

# BROCCOLI RICE

## SERVES 4

3 heads of broccoli (about 900 g), roughly chopped into florets
2 tablespoons coconut oil or good-quality animal fat*
sea salt and freshly ground black pepper

* See Glossary

Place the broccoli in the bowl of a food processor and pulse into tiny, fine pieces that look like rice.

Heat the oil or fat in a large frying pan over medium heat, add the broccoli and cook, stirring occasionally, for 4–5 minutes until tender. Season with salt and pepper and serve.

# CAULIFLOWER RICE

## SERVES 4–6

1 cauliflower, florets and stalk roughly chopped
2 tablespoons coconut oil
sea salt and freshly ground black pepper

Place the cauliflower in the bowl of a food processor and pulse into tiny, fine pieces that look like rice.

Melt the coconut oil in a large frying pan over medium heat. Add the cauliflower and lightly cook for 3–4 minutes until softened. Season with salt and pepper and serve.

# CHICKEN BONE BROTH

## MAKES 3.5–4 LITRES

1–1.5 kg bony chicken parts (I like
to use necks, backs, breastbones
and wings)
2–4 chicken feet (optional)
2 tablespoons apple cider vinegar
1 large onion, roughly chopped
2 carrots, roughly chopped
3 celery stalks, roughly chopped
2 leeks, white part only, roughly
chopped
1 garlic bulb, cut in half horizontally
1 tablespoon black peppercorns,
lightly crushed
2 bay leaves
2 large handfuls of flat-leaf parsley
stalks

Place the chicken pieces in a stockpot, add 5 litres of
cold water and the remaining ingredients and let stand for
1 hour to help draw out the nutrients from the bones.

Place the pot over medium–high heat and bring to the
boil, skimming off the scum that forms on the surface
of the liquid. Reduce the heat to low and simmer for
12–24 hours. The longer you cook the broth, the richer
and more flavourful it will be.

Strain the broth through a fine sieve into a large storage
container, cover and place in the fridge overnight until
the fat rises to the top and congeals. Skim off the fat and
reserve for cooking; it will keep in the fridge for up to
1 week or in the freezer for up to 3 months. Transfer the
broth to smaller airtight containers and place in the fridge
or, for long-term storage, the freezer. The broth can be
stored in the fridge for 3–4 days or freezer for up to
3 months.

# COCONUT FLOUR TORTILLAS

## MAKES 8

3 tablespoons coconut flour
3 tablespoons arrowroot
¼ teaspoon baking powder
½ teaspoon fine sea salt
8 eggwhites from large eggs
2 tablespoons coconut oil

Whisk the coconut flour, arrowroot, baking powder, salt,
eggwhites and 125 ml of water in a large bowl to make
a smooth batter.

Melt 1 teaspoon of the coconut oil in a small frying pan
over medium–high heat. Pour about 3 tablespoons of
batter into the pan. Slightly tilt and swirl the pan to spread
the batter into a thin tortilla, about 13 cm in diameter.
Cook for a few minutes, or until golden brown, then flip
and cook on the other side until lightly golden. Transfer to
a plate and keep warm. Repeat until you have eight tortillas.

# COCONUT YOGHURT

## MAKES ABOUT 1.3 KG

3 tablespoons filtered water
1 tablespoon powdered gelatine*
1.2 litres coconut cream
1 vanilla pod, split and seeds scraped
    (optional)
1–2 tablespoons honey, maple syrup
    or coconut sugar
4 probiotic capsules* or ¼ teaspoon
    vegetable starter culture*

* See Glossary

You'll need a 1.5 litre preserving jar with a lid for this recipe. Wash the jar and all utensils thoroughly in very hot water or run them through a hot rinse cycle in the dishwasher.

Place the filtered water in a small bowl, sprinkle over the gelatine and soak for 2 minutes. Place the coconut cream and vanilla seeds (if using) in a saucepan and gently heat, stirring with a spoon, over medium–low heat until just starting to simmer (90°C, if testing with a thermometer). Do not allow to boil. Immediately remove the pan from the heat. While still hot, mix in the gelatine mixture, then add the sweetener and mix well. Cover the pan with a lid and set aside to cool to lukewarm (35°C or less). Pour 125 ml of the cooled coconut cream mixture into a sterilised bowl. Open the probiotic capsules (if using). Stir the probiotic powder or starter culture into the coconut cream in the bowl. Add the remaining coconut cream and mix well.

Pour the coconut cream mixture into the sterilised jar and loosely seal the lid. Ferment in a warm spot for 12 hours at 38–40°C. To maintain this temperature and allow the yoghurt to culture, wrap the jar in a tea towel and place it on a plate in the oven with the door shut and the oven light on. The light's warmth will keep the temperature consistent. Alternatively, place the tea-towel wrapped jar in an esky, fill a heatproof container with boiling water and place it beside the jar – do not allow them to touch – and close the lid. Replace the boiling water halfway through the fermenting process. Once fermented, the yoghurt tends to form air bubbles and looks as though it has separated. Stir well and refrigerate for at least 10 hours before eating. If it separates after chilling, give it a good whisk. Store in the fridge for up to 2 weeks.

# CRISPY CURRY LEAVES

**MAKES 4 SPRIGS**

150 ml coconut oil
4 curry leaf sprigs
sea salt

Melt the coconut oil in a frying pan over medium heat. Cooking in batches of two sprigs at a time, fry the curry leaves for 4–5 seconds until crisp. Remove with a slotted spoon and drain on paper towel. Season with salt.

# FISH BONE BROTH

**MAKES 3 LITRES**

2 tablespoons coconut oil
2 celery stalks, roughly chopped
2 onions, roughly chopped
1 carrot, roughly chopped
125 ml (½ cup) dry white wine or
    vermouth (optional)
3 or 4 whole, non-oily fish carcasses
    (including heads), such as snapper,
    barramundi or kingfish
3 tablespoons apple cider vinegar
1 handful of thyme sprigs and
    flat-leaf parsley stalks
1 bay leaf

Melt the oil in a stockpot or large saucepan over medium–low heat. Add the vegetables and cook gently for 30–60 minutes until soft. Pour in the wine or vermouth (if using) and bring to the boil. Add the fish carcasses and cover with 3.5 litres of cold water. Stir in the vinegar and bring to the boil, skimming off the scum and any impurities as they rise to the top.

Tie the herbs together with kitchen string and add to the pan. Reduce the heat to low, cover and simmer for at least 3 hours. Remove the fish carcasses with tongs or a slotted spoon and strain the liquid through a sieve into a large storage container. Cover and place in the fridge overnight so that the fat rises to the top and congeals. Remove the fat and reserve it for cooking; it will keep in the fridge for up to 1 week or in the freezer for up to 3 months. Transfer the broth to smaller airtight containers. The broth should be thick and gelatinous – the longer you cook the bones, the more gelatinous it will become. Store in the fridge for 3–4 days or in the freezer for up to 3 months.

# GUACAMOLE

## SERVES 4

2 ½ avocados, diced
1 long red chilli, halved lengthways,
    deseeded and finely chopped,
    plus extra to serve (optional)
juice of 1 lime, plus extra to taste
    (or use the equivalent amount of
    sauerkraut juice)
1 tablespoon finely diced red onion
1 tablespoon chopped coriander leaves
1 tablespoon extra-virgin olive oil
sea salt and freshly ground black pepper

Combine the avocado, chilli, lime juice, onion, coriander and olive oil in a small bowl and gently mix. Season with salt and pepper and sprinkle over the extra chilli (if using). Taste and add a little more lime juice, if you like.

# KALE CHIPS

## SERVES 2

1 bunch of kale (about 350 g)
1 tablespoon coconut oil, melted
½ teaspoon of your favourite spice
    (such as curry powder, ras el
    hanout, smoked paprika, ground
    cumin or ground turmeric)
    (optional)
sea salt

Preheat the oven to 120°C (100°C fan-forced). Line a baking tray with baking paper.

Wash the kale thoroughly in cold water and pat dry. Remove and discard the tough central stems, then cut the leaves into smaller pieces.

In a large bowl, toss the kale with some coconut oil, spice (if using) and salt – go easy on the salt as a little goes a long way. Spread the kale on the baking tray in a single layer; do not overcrowd. Use more than one baking tray, if required. Roast the kale for 35–40 minutes until crispy. Serve immediately or store in an airtight container in the pantry for up to 2 weeks.

# MAYONNAISE

## MAKES ABOUT 500 G

4 egg yolks
2 teaspoons Dijon mustard
1 tablespoon apple cider vinegar
1 tablespoon lemon juice
400 ml olive oil
sea salt and freshly ground
   black pepper

Place the egg yolks, mustard, vinegar, lemon juice, oil and a pinch of salt in a glass jug or jar and blend with a hand-held blender until smooth and creamy, working the blade from the bottom of the jug very slowly up to the top. Season with salt and pepper. Alternatively, place the egg yolks, mustard, vinegar, lemon juice and a pinch of salt in the bowl of a food processor and process until combined. With the motor running, slowly pour in the oil in a thin stream and process until thick and creamy. Season. Store in a sealed glass jar in the fridge for 4–5 days.

# MINT JELLY

## MAKES 600 G

2 granny smith apples, cored and
   chopped, skin on
500 ml (2 cups) filtered water
1 tablespoon lemon juice
2 large handfuls of mint leaves
1½ tablespoons powdered gelatine*
3 tablespoons honey, or to taste

* See Glossary

Place the apple, filtered water, lemon juice and 1 handful of the mint leaves in a saucepan and bring to a simmer. Cook for 10 minutes until the apple is soft. Remove from the heat, add the gelatine and honey and stir until the gelatine dissolves. Allow to cool completely. Place the apple mixture in the bowl of a food processor and blend until smooth. Pass through a fine sieve and discard the leftover pulp.

Finely chop the remaining mint and mix into the apple mixture. Pour into a glass jar, cover and refrigerate for 4 hours, or until set to a wobbly jelly consistency. Give it a good mix before serving.

# NUT-FREE PALEO PASTRY

## MAKES 4 SHEETS

40 g psyllium husks*
100 g coconut flour, plus extra
80g tapioca flour*
3 tablespoons chia seeds
2 tablespoons flaxseeds
40 g pumpkin seeds
3 tablespoons sesame seeds
40 g (¼ cup) sunflower seeds
1½ teaspoons sea salt
3 eggs
3 tablespoons coconut oil, melted

* See Glossary

Place the psyllium husks, coconut and tapioca flour and the seeds in the bowl of a food processor and whiz for a few seconds until the seeds are finely chopped.

Transfer the flour mixture to a large bowl, then mix in the salt. In another bowl, combine 300 ml of water and the eggs and whisk until smooth. Add the coconut oil and the egg mixture to the dry ingredients and mix well to form a wet dough.

Knead the dough on a lightly floured work surface for 1 minute, then divide into two portions and roll into balls. Cover with plastic wrap and rest for another 5 minutes before rolling.

*continued* ❯

Roll out one ball of pastry between two sheets of baking paper, flipping it over and rotating for an even roll, until 3 mm thick. Peel off the top layer of paper and trim the pastry into a large (about 30 cm) square, then cut into two even portions. Cover the pastry sheets with baking paper, then wrap in plastic wrap and place in the fridge until ready to use. Repeat with the remaining ball of dough. Store leftover pastry in the fridge for up to 1 week or in the freezer for up to 3 months.

# PALEO PASTRY

## MAKES 4 SHEETS

150 g almond meal
100 g coconut flour
80 g tapioca flour*
25 g psyllium husks*
1 teaspoon fine sea salt
240 g lard, chilled, cut into
   2.5 cm cubes
125 ml (½ cup) ice-cold water
2 teaspoons apple cider vinegar
2 eggs

* See Glossary

Combine the almond meal, coconut flour, tapioca flour, psyllium husks and salt in a large bowl. Add the lard and, using your fingertips, gently rub it in until it is evenly blended through the dry ingredients.

In a separate bowl, whisk together the water, vinegar and eggs. Pour over the dry ingredients and mix well to form a soft, wet and sticky dough.

Turn the pastry out onto a clean work surface and gently shape into two even balls. Cover with plastic wrap and chill in the fridge for at least 30 minutes.

Roll out one pastry ball between two sheets of baking paper, flipping it over occasionally to work the other side, until 3 mm thick. Place in the freezer for 20 minutes to firm up. Repeat with the second ball.

Once firm, peel off the top layer of paper, trim the pastry into a large (about 30 cm) square, then cut into two even portions. Repeat with the remaining pastry ball. Cover the pastry sheets with baking paper, then wrap in plastic wrap and place in the fridge until ready to use. Store leftover pastry in plastic wrap in the fridge for up to 1 week or in the freezer for up to 3 months.

**Note**
This recipe contains nuts, so may not be suitable for school lunch boxes. For a nut-free paleo pastry, see page 174.

# RAITA

**MAKES 600 G**

½ Lebanese cucumber
200 g Coconut Yoghurt (page 171)
½ teaspoon ground cumin
2 tablespoons finely chopped mint
sea salt and freshly ground
    black pepper

Cut the cucumber in half lengthways and use a teaspoon to scrape out the seeds. Coarsely grate the cucumber flesh and squeeze out the excess liquid with your hands. Combine the cucumber with the yoghurt, cumin and mint in a bowl and stir well. Season to taste and serve.

# RENDERED ANIMAL FAT

**MAKES UP TO 600 G**

1 kg pork back fat, beef fat, lamb fat,
    duck skin or chicken skin (you may
    need to order these in advance
    from your butcher)
125 ml (½ cup) filtered water

If using pork, beef or lamb fat, trim any flesh from the fat with a sharp knife and cut the fat into 2 cm dice.

Place the fat or skin and water in a large heavy-based saucepan over low heat and simmer, stirring occasionally (taking care as the fat may spit), for 3½–4 hours until the water has evaporated and the fat is golden brown and liquefied. Try and keep the fat at around 100°C (use a candy thermometer to test the temperature). You will notice little solid bits of brown crackling floating to the surface and a lot of clear liquid; this is an indication that the fat has rendered and is ready to be taken off the heat.

Allow the rendered fat to cool a little before straining through a fine sieve into a jug, jars, containers or ice-cube trays. Save the leftover crackling bits as they make a delicious snack. The cooled melted fat will be creamy white in colour. Store, covered, in the fridge for up to 3 months or freeze for up to 9 months.

**Tip**
You can also use a slow cooker, as it maintains a gentle heat and works perfectly for rendering fat.

# SAUERKRAUT

## MAKES 1 X 1.5 LITRE JAR

400 g green cabbage
400 g red cabbage
1 beetroot, peeled
2 carrots (about 250 g in total)
1½ teaspoons sea salt
1 sachet vegetable starter culture*
    (this will weigh 2–5 g, depending
    on the brand)

* See Glossary

You will need a 1.5 litre preserving jar with an airlock lid for this recipe. Wash the jar and utensils thoroughly in very hot water. Alternatively, run them through a hot rinse cycle in the dishwasher.

Remove the outer leaves of the cabbages. Choose an unblemished leaf, wash it well and set aside.

Shred the cabbages, beetroot and carrot in a food processor or slice with a knife or mandoline, then transfer to a large glass or stainless steel bowl. Sprinkle the salt over the vegetables, mix well and cover with a plate.

Prepare the starter culture according to the directions on the packet. Add to the vegetables and mix thoroughly.

Using a large spoon, fill the prepared jar with the vegetable mixture, pressing down well to remove any air pockets and leaving 2 cm free at the top. The vegetables should be completely submerged in the liquid. Add more water, if necessary.

Take the clean reserved cabbage leaf, fold it up and place it on top of the vegetables, then add a small glass weight (a shot glass is ideal) to keep everything submerged. Close the lid and wrap a tea towel around the jar to block out the light. Store in a dark place at 16–23°C for 10–14 days. (You can place the jar in an esky to maintain a more consistent temperature.) Different vegetables have different culturing times and the warmer it is, the shorter the time needed. The longer you leave the jar, the higher the level of good bacteria present. It is up to you how long you leave it – some people prefer the tangier flavour that comes with extra fermenting time, while others prefer a milder flavour.

Chill before eating. Once opened, the sauerkraut will last for up to 2 months in the fridge when kept submerged in liquid. If unopened, it will keep for up to 9 months in the fridge. Don't throw out the brine – it can be used to make a delicious dressing.

# SEMI-DRIED TOMATOES

**MAKES 350 G**

500 g cherry tomatoes, halved
sea salt and freshly ground
   black pepper
1½ teaspoons dried oregano
100 ml extra-virgin olive oil

Preheat the oven to 120°C (100°C fan-forced).
Line a baking tray with baking paper and place a wire
rack on the tray.

Arrange the cherry tomatoes, cut-side up, on the wire rack.
Season the tomatoes with salt and pepper and sprinkle on
the dried oregano. Bake in the oven for 1½ hours, or until
the tomatoes are dry around the edges but still soft in the
centre. Set aside to cool completely. Transfer the tomatoes
to a sterilised glass jar, pour in the olive oil, seal and store in
the fridge for up to 2 weeks.

# SMOKED BARBECUE SAUCE

**MAKES 420 G**

100 g tomato paste
3 tablespoons apple cider vinegar
1 tablespoon Dijon mustard
120 g honey
100 ml maple syrup
½ teaspoon smoked paprika
100 ml tamari or coconut aminos*
2 garlic cloves, finely chopped
1½ tablespoons liquid smoke
   (optional) (see Note)
pinch of ground cloves
1 cinnamon stick
sea salt (optional)

* See Glossary

Place all the ingredients in a saucepan, mix well and bring
to a simmer. Turn the heat to low and cook for 10 minutes.
Allow to cool and season with salt, if desired.

Leftover barbecue sauce can be stored in an airtight
container in the fridge for up to 2 weeks.

**Note**
Liquid smoke is a water-soluble liquid that forms from
condensed smoke particles when chips from a hardwood
(such as hickory) are burned. You can purchase liquid
smoke from some supermarkets, delis, specialty food
stores or online.

# SWEET POTATO PUREE

**MAKES 280–300 G**

1 sweet potato (about 470 g)

Preheat the oven to 200°C (180°C fan-forced). Line a baking tray with baking paper.

Prick the sweet potato with a fork a few times, place on the prepared tray and roast for 60–70 minutes until tender. When cool enough to handle, peel away the skin and discard. With a potato masher, mash the sweet potato until very smooth; alternatively, place in the bowl of a food processor and process until smooth.

# TERIYAKI SAUCE

**MAKES 200 ML**

125 ml (½ cup) tamari or
    coconut aminos*
40 g (¼ cup) coconut sugar
3 tablespoons honey
2 teaspoons finely grated garlic
1 teaspoon finely grated ginger
1½ teaspoons tapioca flour*

* See Glossary

Mix the tamari or coconut aminos with 3 tablespoons of water and the sugar, honey, garlic and ginger in a small saucepan and place over medium heat. Bring to the boil, reduce the heat to low and gently simmer for 5 minutes to dissolve the sugar and allow the flavours to develop.

Meanwhile, mix the tapioca flour and 1 tablespoon of water together until combined.

Bring the tamari mixture to the boil, then pour in the tapioca mixture. Stir constantly until thickened and the sauce coats the back of the spoon. Remove from the heat. Allow to cool, then strain, discarding the ginger and garlic pulp. Store in an airtight glass bottle in the fridge for up to 4 weeks.

# TOMATO KETCHUP

## MAKES 330 G

180 g tomato paste
100 ml filtered water (add more
    water if you prefer the sauce
    to be thinner)
1 tablespoon apple cider vinegar
1 teaspoon garlic powder
1 teaspoon onion powder
½ teaspoon ground cinnamon
¼ teaspoon freshly grated nutmeg
1 teaspoon honey
pinch of ground cloves

Mix the tomato paste and water in a small saucepan, place over medium heat and bring to a simmer (add more water if necessary). Remove from the heat and stir in the remaining ingredients until incorporated. Cool and store in an airtight glass jar in the fridge for up to 4 weeks.

# WORCESTERSHIRE SAUCE

## MAKES 150 ML

125 ml (½ cup) apple cider vinegar
2 tablespoons filtered water
2½ tablespoons tamari or
    coconut aminos*
½ teaspoon ground ginger
½ teaspoon mustard powder
½ teaspoon onion powder
½ teaspoon garlic powder
¼ teaspoon ground cinnamon
¼ teaspoon freshly ground
    black pepper

* See Glossary

Combine all the ingredients in a saucepan. Bring to the boil over medium heat, stirring occasionally. Reduce the heat to low and simmer for 10 minutes. Remove from the heat and allow to cool. Store in an airtight glass bottle in the fridge for up to 4 weeks.

Right: Sauerkraut, page 177

# GLOSSARY

## ACTIVATED SEEDS AND NUTS

Nuts and seeds are a great source of healthy fats, but they contain phytic acid, which binds to minerals so that they can't be readily absorbed. Activating nuts and seeds lessens the phytates, making minerals easier to absorb. Activated nuts and seeds are available from health-food stores. To make your own, simply soak the nuts in filtered water (12 hours for hard nuts, such as almonds; 4–6 hours for softer nuts, such as cashews and macadamias). Rinse the nuts, then spread out on a baking tray and place in a 50°C oven or dehydrator to dry out. This will take anywhere from 6 to 24 hours, depending on the temperature and the kind of nuts or seeds. Store in an airtight container in the pantry for up to 3 months.

## COCONUT AMINOS

Made from coconut sap, coconut aminos is similar in flavour to a light soy sauce. Because it is free of both soy and gluten, it makes a great paleo alternative to soy sauce and tamari. Coconut aminos is available at health-food stores.

## COCONUT OIL

Coconut oil has a high smoke point, making it great for cooking at high temperatures. The viscosity of coconut oil changes depending on the temperature and ranges from liquid to solid. Although coconut oil is high in saturated fats, they are mainly medium-chain saturated fatty acids, which means the body can use them quickly and does not have to store them. Coconut oil is available from supermarkets. Look for virgin cold-pressed varieties, as these have had the least amount of processing.

## COLLAGEN POWDER, GRASS-FED

Collagen is a protein found in bones, skin and connective tissue, which breaks down into amino acids. The amino acids are then absorbed and used as building blocks that support collagen production and healing throughout the body. Collagen powder can be found online or at pharmacies or health-food stores. I always choose powdered collagen sourced from organic, grass-fed beef.

## GELATINE

Gelatine is the cooked form of collagen (see above). I always choose gelatine sourced from organic, grass-fed beef. Vegetarian substitutes for gelatine include agar agar and carrageen, which are made from two different types of seaweed. Sometimes these aren't as strong as regular gelatine, so you may need to increase the quantity. Some kosher gelatines are also vegan. You can buy gelatine made from organic, grass-fed beef, agar agar and carrageen from health-food stores or online.

## GOOD-QUALITY ANIMAL FAT

I use either coconut oil or good-quality animal fats for cooking as they have high smoke points (meaning they do not oxidise at high temperatures). Some of my favourite animal fats to use are lard (pork fat), tallow (rendered beef fat), rendered chicken fat and duck fat. These may be hard to find – ask at your local butcher or meat supplier, look online for meat suppliers who sell them or make your own (see page 176).

## JARRED FISH

I buy preserved fish – such as tuna, salmon, mackerel and sardines – in jars rather than cans, due to the presence of Bisphenol A (BPA) in many cans. BPA is a toxic chemical that can interfere with our hormonal system. You can find jarred fish at specialty food-stores and supermarkets.

## LIQUID CHLOROPHYLL

Chlorophyll is the green pigment in plants that helps trap light energy from the sun. It is known as a 'blood builder' and aids in blood clotting, balancing hormones, skin and wound healing, and also plays a role in detoxification and digestion. It has also been used as a weight-loss aid. When you eat green leafy veggies, you ingest chlorophyll in plant form, but adding liquid chlorophyll to a smoothie or juice is a quick and convenient way to boost your health.

## NORI SHEETS

Nori is a dark green, paper-like, toasted seaweed used in Japanese dishes. Nori provides an abundance of essential nutrients and is rich in vitamins, iron and other minerals, amino acids, omega-3 and omega-6, and antioxidants. Nori sheets are commonly used to roll sushi, but they can also be added to salads, soups and many other dishes. You can buy nori sheets from Asian grocers and most supermarkets.

## POMEGRANATE MOLASSES

Pomegranate molasses is a thick, tangy and glossy reduction of pomegranate juice that is rich in antioxidants. Pomegranate molasses is used in Middle Eastern countries for glazing meat and chicken before roasting, and in sauces, salad dressings and marinades. You can buy it from Middle Eastern grocers and some delis.

## PROBIOTIC CAPSULES

Probiotic capsules contain live bacteria that can help to regulate digestion, clear up yeast infections and assist with conditions such as irritable bowel syndrome. These capsules need to be kept in the fridge. They can be swallowed whole, or opened up and used to ferment drinks such as kefir. Probiotic capsules can be found at pharmacies and health-food stores.

## PSYLLIUM HUSK

Psyllium is a gluten-free, soluble fibre that is used to maintain intestinal health, as the high fibre content absorbs excess liquid in the gut. When exposed to liquids, the husks swell up to create a gel. It is therefore important to drink plenty of fluids when consuming psyllium. Psyllium products can be found at health-food stores.

## SALT

I use sea salt or Himalayan (pink) salt in my cooking, as they are less processed than table salt, contain more minerals and have a lovely crunchy texture. You can buy both types at supermarkets and health-food stores.

## SUMAC

Sumac is a spice made from red sumac berries that have been dried and crushed. It has antimicrobial properties and a tangy, lemony flavour, which makes it ideal for pairing with seafood. It's also delicious in salad dressings.

## TAPIOCA FLOUR

Tapioca flour is made by grinding up the dried root of the manioc (also known as cassava) plant. It can be used to thicken dishes or in gluten-free baking. You can find tapioca flour at health-food stores and some supermarkets.

## VEGETABLE STARTER CULTURE

A vegetable starter culture is used to kickstart the fermentation process when culturing vegetables and yoghurts. I use a broad-spectrum starter sourced from organic vegetables rather than one grown from dairy sources. Vegetable starter culture usually comes in sachets and can be purchased at health-food stores or online. You can also get fresh, non-dairy starter cultures for yoghurt and kefir.

# THANKS

Endless gratitude to my divine family, especially my sweet wife, Nic. Thank you, angel, for being your authentic self and for sharing your nurturing and down-to-earth way of being with us all. Your loving support and insightful input is beyond a gift, and this journey we're sharing is, as you know, absolutely epic! And my two extraordinary daughters, Chilli and Indii, you're both ever-so inspiring, unique and astounding in every way. Every day with you both is an absolute blast of pure fun, and it surely is a cosmic pleasure to be your old man!

To the wonder twins, Monica and Jacinta Cannataci, you both bring so much pure goodness and passion to everything that you do in life, and I'm so proud and heartily thankful to be able to share this journey with you both. You're hands-down, without a doubt THE DREAM TEAM!

To the incredible photography and styling team of Steve Brown, Deb Kaloper, William Meppem, Mark Roper and Lucy Tweed, you are all such gifted artists and the delicious essence you all passionately add just brings all of my recipes to life. I wish you all my heartfelt thanks.

To Ingrid Ohlsson and Mary Small, thank you for believing in the message of real food and for believing in me. I appreciate your support tremendously.

A big thanks to Clare Marshall, for your eye for detail and for making sure that everything is A-OK!

To Charlotte Ree, thank you for being your vibrant self, and for being an incredible publicist. You are an absolute gem!

To Megan Johnston, thank you so very much for your meticulous editing.

To Emily O'Neill, thank you for your colourful imagination and for creating such a beautiful design for this book.

A loving thanks to my super mum, Joy. Mum, you have always been a brilliant source of inspiration for me and I'm so very grateful for all that you do and the joyful love that you shine. I'm very proud to be your son!

I also wish to express a mountain of appreciation and love for my many profoundly inspiring and truly marvellous teachers, mentors and friends for their pioneering work, and for their guidance on this exquisite journey called life. Your conscious contribution means the world to me: Nora Gedgaudas and Lisa Collins, Trevor Hendy, Rudy Eckhardt, Dr Pete Bablis, Dr David Perlmutter, Dr Kelly Brogan, Dr William Davis, Dr Joseph Mercola, Dave Asprey, Helen Padarin, Dr Libby, Prof. Tim Noakes, Pete Melov, Dr Martha Herbert, Dr Natasha Campbell-McBride, Dr Alessio Fasano, Dr Datis Kharrazian, Dr Ron Rosedale and the late Weston A. Price ... to name a few.

And last, but certainly not least, I wish to say thank you to YOU, for being you!

# INDEX

**A PLUM BOOK**

First published in 2018 by
Pan Macmillan Australia Pty Limited
Level 25, 1 Market Street,
Sydney, NSW 2000, Australia

Level 3, 112 Wellington Parade,
East Melbourne, VIC 3002, Australia

Design by Emily O'Neill
Edited by Megan Johnston
Index by Jo Rudd
Photography by Steve Brown, William Meppem, Rob Palmer
    and Mark Roper
Prop and food styling by Deborah Kaloper and Lucy Tweed
Food preparation by Jacinta and Monica Cannataci
Typeset by Emily O'Neill
Colour reproduction by Splitting Image Colour Studio
Printed and bound in China by 1010 Printing International Limited

A CIP catalogue record for this book is available
from the National Library of Australia.

We advise that the information contained in this
book does not negate personal responsibility on
the part of the reader for their own health and
safety. It is recommended that individually tailored
advice is sought from your healthcare or medical
professional. The publishers and their respective
employees, agents and authors are not liable for
injuries or damage occasioned to any person as
a result of reading or following the information
contained in this book.

The publisher would like to thank the following for
their generosity in providing props for the book:
Bentoland, Big W, Biome, Happy Tiffin, Kmart,
Muji, Smash Enterprises, Target, Thermo Boutique
and Thermos.

10 9 8 7 6